THE CASE OF A
NURSING FATHER

THE CASE OF A NURSING FATHER

SYLVESTER ODION AKHAINE

PARTRIDGE

To order additional copies of this book, contact
Toll Free 0800 990 914 (South Africa)
+44 20 3014 3997 (outside South Africa)
orders.africa@partridgepublishing.com

www.partridgepublishing.com/africa

CONTENTS

DEDICATION

To my mother who gave her all

FOREWORD

A Celebration of Humanism

The destiny of the Nigerian state may aptly be described as that of a revolution in waiting. Radical intellectuals and activists schooled in the Marxist-Leninist ideology have, in the last five decades, identified pre-revolutionary symptoms in the country's setting.

The author of *The Case of a Nursing Father*, Dr. Sylvester Odion Akhaine, turns fifty this year, the very year that splits in half a century of the troubled ' existence' of Nigeria. He belongs to the generation that feels the full existential impact of those social traits that recommend the country for a revolution.

As such, domesticated as the title of this books may appear, the reader cannot but find in it filtrates of his ideological disposition, against the backdrop of the struggle for radical transformation as a national desideratum.

Generally, this book is a pot-pourri of incidences, encounters and reflections presented in stories selected mainly from the journalistic writings of Odion Akhaine.

He writes about the family in the title-story, of his self-appointed role as a nanny to avail his wife the opportunity to pursue her medical career to the fullest without the promptings of any affirmative action. Later, he laments the death of his mother in an emotion laden mix of prose and poetry. Both experiences have ideological underpinnings concerning the woman as a pillar.

So do his narratives and commentaries on the cosmopolitan world, on the British monarchy, the Obama factor in contemporary politics of the United States, the ambiguity of the African personality in an iniquitous global order. The author feels the tortuous blizzard of the winter in London as he frowns at the humiliation of Nigerians, himself inclusive, at the airports of metropolitan cities. To the one he must adapt and the other he must reject.

Where the political culture agrees with his ideological chemistry he celebrates. Cuba offers an appropriate turf for such a celebration. His visit to Castro's country evoked exciting reminiscences of the revolutionary process that he would normally prescribe for any country, like Nigeria, held hostage by the rapacity of dictators.

His 'Cuban Notes' titillates the mind with the exploits of Fidel Castro, Che Guevara, Camilo Cienfuegos and other heroes of the revolution as well as the popular will that gives meaning to their feats.

In the same breath, *The Case of a Nursing Father*, even by the expository passages on Cuba, the Netherlands and a host of other countries, has the trappings of a travelogue. The 500-year-old Yoruba community in Cuba is given a treatment that is both entertaining and instructive. So instructive is it that the author spares a few lines for a comparative analysis of the cultural reality of the Yoruba heritage in Cuba and what currently obtains in Osun State in Nigeria.

Last, but not least, one aspect of this book that will continue to challenge future generation of Nigerians is its dedication to real heroism. Perhaps a further demonstration of the true identities of the heroes of Nigerian nationalism as articulated in Festus Iyayi's award-winning novel, HEROES, is the series of requiems in prose recorded by Dr. Odion Akhaine in *The Case of a Nursing Father.*

Their names roll out like martyrs that they are in the circumstance of social struggle. Some of them, like Chief Anthony Enahoro and Comrade Baba Omojola passed on as senior citizens consummated in their nationalistic passion. Others, like Comrade Olaitan Oyerinde, the late Personal Secretary to the Edo State Governor, Comrade Adams Oshiomole, were actually brought down by the assassin's bullet.

The reader will appreciate their heroic virtue as extolled by the author from an intimate, authoritative perspective. And this is one strong point about the book; that the author is not leading the reader through a narcissistic excursion, but the celebration of humanism in a most altruistic manner.

Ben Tomoloju,
Lagos, April 5, 2014.

OPEN LETTER TO THE AUTHOR

Today is your 50th birthday. I join members of your family and friends in wishing you long life and good health. Health is wealth. You decided to celebrate your anniversary by releasing, today, a collection of essays straddling literary fictions, History, cultures and deep philosophic thoughts. Some of them have been published in respected tabloids here in Nigeria and others abroad.

This book contains apparently "strange" co-existing essays, because they belong to different genres. Your innovative style may, perhaps, not be understood by those who don't have a multiple disciplinary intellectual tradition stipulating that one can assemble a collection of different essays into a complex structure called body of knowledge. Note the concept, "body of knowledge".

In concrete terms, all parts of the human body, are inextricably linked by nerves and blood. Fluid, the blood, passes through nerves, the vessels. All parts of the body are equally indispensable. They relate to one another from birth to death!

I want to conceptualize your collection of essays, by borrowing a term called faction, a concept popularised by Odia Ofeimun with whom I studied a course, Political Philosophy, under late Professor Billy Dudley, a distinguished scholar at the University of Ibadan.

Permit me this important but useful digression which is also relevant in the subsequent analysis of your wonderful essays. In Billy Dudley's class, we were only six students, other colleagues deliberately avoided his courses, like Ebola Fever, because if you are not willing to accept the fact that all disciplines are, more or less, interrelated in what is known as body of knowledge, then you have to quickly go and register for courses like, History of local governments in Nigeria.

Those of us who took the risk to register for Professor Billey Dudley's courses were also convinced he would have applied the same concept "body of knowledge to teach" the History of local government in Nigeria. And of course some students would have, as expected, gone into intellectual exile within the campus, may be in the name of intellectual tsunami, i.e. seaside volcanic outbreak.

Still on Billy Dudley, a Nigerian and an Itsekiri from the old Bendel State, used to teach a course, ethnicity in Nigeria. In his lectures he made use of physics, mathematics, anthropology, political economy, sociology and political theories to explain, coherently, ethnicity in our country. He patiently entertained questions and answered them convincingly.

One would ask here, what is the relevance of Billy Dudley's model and your collection of essays? I see a similar model from the first essay" *The case of a Nursing Father*" to the last one, "*Beyond Whispers, Baba Goes Home*". Between these two chapters are essays which reflect your complex experiences and the way your globalised visions interact with other human beings from your village, Emaudo, old Bendel State now Edo State in Esan land to cities and towns in Nigeria and abroad. To put it succinctly, you are a permanent student of life on this earth and your experiences are your permanent teachers! This paradigm applies to all of us.

Many people do not know that you are also a creative writer to wit: *Our Colony* (1998), *Another Woman of Substance* (2000) and *The Next Anarchy* (2008).

Doctor, as I fondly call you often, this open letter is a review of *The Case of the Nursing Father*. I don't want to undertake the classical and traditional reviews to which we are used in this kind of occasion. As an unpleasant non-conformist, known as *Omo Wole Soyinka*, in Yoruba i.e. Soyinka's disciple, which I am, I will proceed to take look at issues in your essays. I must quickly add here, that I will not bore you with what I called snoring details. However, I will build upon your essays by extrapolating and amplifying them.

Everybody has a right and liberty to interpret them through, in his / her binocular lenses. This is the beauty of intellectual diversity and contradictory views of Wo(man) kind and Nature. Without contradictions and dialectical discourses grounded upon facts and figures, there will never have occurred constructive and destructive human progress, evolution and development. Human thoughts conceptualized and developed electricity, African music and dance (positive) and also atomic/hydrogen bombs and cannibalism (negative).

With regards to your essays, I will dwell on what I consider issues affecting all of us. I must quickly add here, that in all your essays, the subject matters you raised concern all of us. You described the beauty and the ugliness of human behaviour. For lack of space, I plead with the audience and yourself to allow me spend some time on some of the crucial issues you highlighted.

Two essays set me thinking about the future and fate of Human Beings and the planet. These essays are: "A Requiem for Bullet Stoner", and "For Carlos Fuentes and Olaitan Oyerinde". In the former essay, I quote, "Each time I reflect on life on this earth, with all the daily toils, I marvel about its meaning. Life on earth is a reality that we cannot change until Armageddon occurs whether in the prophetic way as in the holy writ or through the destructive acts of man. Today, the split atoms in the arsenal of the superpowers can destroy the home of man over and over again. We are already reaping the consequence of mother earth through man's emission of greenhouse gases. The struggle is between light and darkness. The capacity to overcome the dark recesses of one's being, beaming light on it in ways that enhance the humanity of others, is perhaps the pearl of life. It does not lie in the overwhelming acquisition of the material things of life".

You must have reached a moment of intellectual crisis within yourself when you put down these thoughts. I cannot re-invent the wheel. Not possible. Let me add some modest value to your thoughts here. This is a proof that you understand the concept called "body of knowledge". You are able to understand the consequences of human beings in their aggressive nature to acquire material wealth at the expense of happiness. Second, you also know, through my interactions with you, that for the first time in the History of Mankind, human beings have over-produced material things and at the same time, prices of these goods keep rising artificially.

Two American Nobel laureates in economic science have written extensively on the economic consequences of the looming ecological disaster unfolding itself before our very eyes. Joseph Stiglitz, *Globalization and its Discontents* (2002), *The Price of*

Inequality (2012) and; Paul Krugman, *End this Depression Now* (2012) and *Oligarchs and Money* (cf. New York Times, April 6, 2014).

These two world renowned experts confirmed that the prices of raw materials and finished goods are artificially maintained so that those who own the means of production would not close down their factories and farms. It is not a hidden secret that about 40 percent of food produced in developed countries are deliberately destroyed to preserve artificial prices. In some cases, armored tanks escort food bullions to the dumping sites with a view to destroying food stuffs which should have been consumed by hungry human beings in all parts of the world.

Both J. Stiglitz and Paul Krugman confirm that there are trillions of dollars lying idle in safe havens in some islands all over the world. If these monies, a perfect symbol of unprecedented human wealth, they insist, attract just ten percent taxation, most of the public and private debts in both developed and underdeveloped would be considerably reduced. You also know that 8.2 million citizens are homeless in European Union and there are 8.4 million houses unoccupied!

In line with the thoughts of these American intellectuals, you called our attention to prevailing socio-economic crisis of USA. Titled *"For Carlos Fuentes and Olaitan Oyerinde "*, you brought out the salient remarks of late Carlos Fuentes, the great Mexican writer who warned that the collapse of what he aptly called ossified socialism, i.e. absence of self-criticism, does not mean that the collapse of Soviet Union, ushered in peace and prosperity in the world. He warned, "The US, so intent on finding enemies outside its borders that suit their Manichean script of its historical record will have to deal with its internal enemies. Among them : the lack of women's rights, ecological ruin, educational bankruptcy, the drying up of funds for scientific research, crumbling bridges and roads, blighted cities in the throes of drugs and violence, the plight of the elderly and the homeless, the millions living under the 'poverty line'"

Your visit to Cuba was captured in the essay, "Cuban Notes". This is a country whose source of income is sugar cane. Despite, the American embargo since 1960 till date, the Cuban leadership was able to mobilize its resources to establish one of the best education, training and health programmes in the world. United Nations attests to this fact. Thousands of Cuban doctors are in Africa and Latin America.

Recent events have shown that a country does not necessarily have to create a socialist state, in order to commence development. South Korea, a non- socialist country, has devoted over 48 percent of her resources to education and training within 30 years. Thus, she is now the 7th largest economy in the world.

When you listen to debate in the current National Conference here in our country, delegates haggle over resources control. They fail to realize that, to put an end to what Professor Itse Sagay calls the irresponsible feeding bottle fiscal federalism, in all its ramifications, the best resource control is in the development of human resources via education and training of each federating units of Nigeria. Each of these units must spend at least UNESCO's recommended 26 % of its annual budget on education and training.

Doctor, let me seize the opportunity to remind you of our eternal debates over the future of Nigeria in this 21st century driven by knowledge economy. This country will soon be relevant or irrelevant in the comity of nations if it decides or refuses to spend a huge substantial sum of her resources in education and training. Human beings and not raw materials are the real engines of development. Japan does not have raw materials but she has massively invested in her citizens via education and training.

I can now understand why you ruminated over Nigeria's problems when you were about to leave Cuba in that your essay, *"Cuban Notes"*: "… and the Cuban reverie were taken over by the Nigerian blues- Boko Haram, Kidnappers, power outage, government by committees".

Before I take leave of this Cuban *wahala*, I noticed you made mention of the portraits of great leaders adorning the Revolutionary Square, in Havana. Amongst them is Eduardo de Santos, the "eternal president of Angola"; eternal in the sense that he has been in power for the past 33 years.

Two issues about Dos Santos. First, one of his biggest "achievements" was making his daughter Isabel Dos Santos, the richest woman billionaire in Africa. According to America's *Forbes* Magazine her assets are put at US$3 billion. Two, a journalist described her wedding in the following terms, "the wedding ceremony cost about US$ 4 million, with a special choir flown in from Belgium and two planes chartered to bring food from France. About 800 guests were present at the wedding, half of them relatives of the couple".

At the same time, the vast majority of Angolans live below poverty line. And in the 70's some Nigerian students died, were jailed and expelled from the universities in the real name of supporting Dos Santos liberation movement, MPLA with the slogan "A luta continua, vitória é certa"! What an irony.

Let us painfully move on. In most of your essays you paid glowing tributes to some Nigerian youths who lost their lives in the course of fighting for social justice and political liberation. I am sure that those who have taken over from them will always remember you for documenting their sacrifices.

I will describe you as a humanist. You care for the old men and women. A dwindling culture amongst our Nigerian youth eaten up by the culture of selfishness and greed. You gave a particular attention to the inability of Chief Anthony Enahoro, a Nigerian hero, to afford decent medical care. One of your younger colleagues had to send him drugs regularly from Germany! In the same vein, Baba Omojola, a great Nigerian intellectual could not live decently because he was neglected by the ruling predatory class who hated him for his ideals!

Kindly pardon me if I have not done justice to all the issues you dealt with in your essays which I read four times before writing this non-conformist review.

To conclude let me make these observations. First, you write well. Writing and reading culture is dying even with some members of your generation. Two, you care for human beings. Your writings indicate to me that you are part of the human species that would prevent this selfish world from degenerating into anarchy and barbarism. Finally, I want to pay a glowing tribute to Aina, your loving and hardworking wife who kept the home and supported you in the face of hardship and deprivation engineered by those who hated you because of your collective fight for social justice.

I am proud of you.
Yours Sincerely,
Tunde Fatunde.
April 12, 2014.

AUTHOR'S NOTE

A reader of *The Case of a Nursing Father* would come across twenty-two tales. They include *The Case of a Nursing Father* (the title of the volume); *Mother, Season of Ceremonies*; *My Easter Trip to the Netherlands*; *Washington Post-Inauguration*; *Many Wishes of Xmas and New Year*; *Christmas without Ponmo*; *Is This Virus Deadlier than Aids?*; *Sex and Soccer*; *The Dress Code of a Socialist, Cuban Notes*; *Che Guevara: Twenty-Eight Years after the Mortal October*; *Bloodbath at Bayero*; *The Days of the Dracula*; *What a Country*; *The Story of Holly and Jessica*; *The Virgin Nightmare*; *If They Play Jazz in Heaven, Play on Dizzy*; *For Carlos Fuentes and Olaitan Oyerinde*; *Just To Say Good Bye*; *Requiem for Bullet Stoner*; *A Tribute to a Brave Couple and Beyond Whispers, Baba Goes Home*.

These stories were written between 1993 and 2015. In the presentation of the narratives I was faced with two choices. Firstly, present them sequentially according to the time in which each tale was written. And secondly, arrange them thematically. I chose the latter because, it makes for interesting reading to read the tales on the basis of theme. Besides, it has the added value of run-on effect.

However, it is important to note that an attempt was made to publish this volume in 2014 under the Panaf imprint, the work had to be withdrawn from circulation due to avoidable editorial errors for which I was responsible. However, four new stories, namely, *Christmas without Ponmo, Che Guevara: Twenty-Eight Years after the Mortal October, The Days of the Dracula* and *What a Country* have been added to this volume.

I

THE CASE OF A NURSING FATHER

[THE GUARDIAN, JANUARY 4, 1999]

WHEN my boy, baby Omata arrived on October 29 last year, his mum and I were overwhelmed with joy. Before his arrival, I had always dreaded the prospect of having to join the middle class slave deals which produce child labourers and slaves in the name of housemaids who are ordered around by the lady of the house. My own cousin who lives in Port Harcourt brought into his household a maid. She was very young and up and doing with the domestic chores. Co-habiting with him was his youngest brother, Lucky who was in primary school. Each morning, unbeknown to my cousin, the maid would watch Lucky prepare: have a bath, shine his pair of sandals, fill his water can and don on his miniature hold-all bag and then depart for school. It should have been obvious that there was something suspicious about such a behaviour. One morning, she woke up with a sour countenance. It was time to bid farewell to domestic slavery. She packed her bag and baggage ready to go. My cousin asked her what the matter was. She looked shy but determined. She said she wanted to go to school like Lucky. My cousin felt a twinge down in him. He couldn't say a word. Not that he had a choice anyway but he allowed her to live out her destiny. In his inside, which had some measure of the same nature of insurrection, apologies to William Shakespeare, he realised how he had been a twentieth century slave driver. These sorts of feeling are what make us human, not the business orientation and mindedness which could have made him say: afterall, I paid for her service.

Although my wife was toying with the idea of a housemaid in her discussions with friends, my countenance each time I chanced on such discussion spoke volumes; those who have them and have had them before know what the stories are: Some

3

women eager for housemaids have had their matrimonial homes shattered by the maids. In those circumstances, the delicate constitution of some of the housemaids nurtured by the regular square meals of the homes they tended had with time had the men with equally delicate passion on the floor. Hmm! Isn't my wife lucky that I am opposed to them? Also, numerous instances abound of housemaids who beat to stupor the kids under their care. Others simply allowed the kids to overwork their lachrymal glands to the point of running temperature. These are still prevalent practices today; mind you, they are just minor cases. Worst cases abound when you probe further. This is not to deny, however, the existence of a tiny colony of saints among them. I could appreciate my wife's grounds for toying with the idea; a working class woman she is: She has to keep her job and retain her growing band of clientelle. My mind was made up assisting her in taking care of Omati Bobo as we fondly call our baby, more so as I have a liberal work regime as an activist.

The routine is: On week days I stay with Bobo taking care to shift all my appointments in the office to afternoon. His mum who now keeps adjusted working hours—from 9 a.m. to 2 p.m. and sometimes from 9 a.m. to 3 p.m. on work days—comes in to relieve me, always in the nick of time, enabling me to begin my afternoon schedules. I do this without giving much thought to societal expectations or cultural norms of the African world view system even though the socio-political questions of feminism, gender and/or sexism cannot be totally overlooked and as such play themselves up in mind. Thus I ask myself: when women talk about being oppressed and not being valorised, and ask for equality and stuff like that, is this what they mean? Does this extend to not being assisted in all spheres of marital responsibilities and the lack of equity in man-woman interrelationship within a broader societal context? Well, I have found my own forward looking strategy (FLS), my affirmative action. Mind you, I was not in Beijing and need not be, to know that equity is equity whether in the home or work place. Therefore, in our deconstruction crusade against patriarchal values, we must not forget that every society has values, which constitute its stabilising factor. Based on these values, we must remember that western universalism of their individualistic value is a threat to African communal ethos which advocates mutual help and is never antithetical to it no matter the giver or the recipient.

Come to think about my present routine, there is abundant joy in caring for children. As I was writing this piece, Bobo tried to grab the sheets of paper being used and tear them to shreds. A child's innocence can be infectious. No wonder of them, Jesus said "allow little children to come to me for theirs is the kingdom of God". He has just excreted on my laps and I have received three doses of urine earlier. I can tell the motive of every of his cries. This time he wants to eat. Next it would sleep and at another, heat. The only thing I lack in taking care of my boy is the mammary glands. I think someone should begin a cloning campaign here.

II

MOTHER

[THE GUARDIAN, JANUARY 5, 2007]

IMAGINE you were at a wedding ceremony of one of your younger siblings in company of your mother, mother of the groom. First, she was at the traditional wedding ceremony where she led a horde of other women to add colour to the occasion. You greeted her as wont a child—routinely. Next you sat among the numerous participants. In a moment of realisation, you passed some crispy naira notes to her through your spouse in case she wanted to fete her in-laws in a show of conviviality and gratitude for giving their daughter in marriage. That was over and you saw her leave for home. You did not see her in camera and say goodbye because you knew you would for sure see her the next day at the church wedding rites. Truly, she was at the church the next day. She again played her role as mother of the groom in the holy matrimony. While the service lasted, you had the rare privilege of photographing her with the zeal and agility of some paparazzi. After the church rituals she moved among many others to the reception. There she sat at the high table, played the vintage mother and watched the final marriage rite of her son who had now moved into familyhood. At last, she left. You did not have a word with her; you merely saw her off and apprised her of your plans for departure to your own destination the succeeding day. 'Tomorrow is always there,' you reasoned inside you. Due to human weakness, you did not consider that though tomorrow is always there, it may not be there fully for you.

Everyone saw your mother spick-and-span in those two successive days of the marriage ceremony. As a son, unlike others, you had noticed in your mum the absence of a certain vive, that which hints of life at its peak. Your fears were then reinforced when your aunt, younger by a couple of years than your mother, told you of her readings of your mother's health, insisting that you should pay more attention to her health. Aside, out of filial worry, you told your spouse of your plan to take your mother home for a medical check-up. This worry lingered on and on, and you confided to your spouse as often as the feeling arose.

In the middle of work in your office on the succeeding Thursday after the marriage ritual which had held the previous weekend, a call came through to one of your siblings who coincidentally was in your office and the voice on the other end announced, grief-torn and rudely, that your mother was dead, your own mother, the woman you saw 'hale and hearty' barely five days before. In the midst of shock and confusion, you put a call across to the source of the sorrowful news to verify the truth of the matter; the reasons being unbelief, and the fact that you had a grandmother who had spent almost a century in a rare display of longevity and you had to ask if her mortal passage, the one being anticipated was the actual news. You got 'no' for an answer. The truth of the matter, you were told in a manner bereft of all guiles, was that your biological mother was no more.

You then requested to know what happened—precisely what killed her. Afterall, man and woman must die of something. You were told an idyllic tale of her exit: she woke up on the fateful day, went to the farm (she was a subsistence farmer and petty trader) and came back to cook her meals and attend a meeting (thrift society) which was holding in your father's parlour. She offered kolanut to members of the society in profuse appreciation for their being present at her son's wedding. She ate her share of the kolanut, sat down and shortly slumped. One of her daughters-in-law who sat close to her raised alarm and she was then rushed to the hospital. By the time, the medical doctor had time to feel her pulse, she was certified dead. That was my mother, Mrs. Victoria Akhaine (nee Omoike). She passed on December 7, 2006 at the age of 64.

One thing about death is its surprising nature. My mother's death shocked me to the marrow and it hurts so much as I had yet to give back something reasonable and worthwhile enough for her labour in bringing forth and keeping my siblings and I alive. Come to think of it, she had actually bid me goodbye when less than a month ago before her death she had told me to remain the 'dustbin' of her family, absorbing the wrongs of my siblings with stoic calmness. Besides, she sent me photographs of her baptism into the catholic faith with the message: "You may not know where life's road will lead you. Keep moving. God is walking with you—Sweet Mama."

My mother is gone forever and forever. But I remember her in the memorable lines of Ann Taylor's (1782-1866) *My Mother*:

Who fed me from her gentle breast,
And hush'd me in her arms to rest,
And on my cheek sweet kisses prest?
My Mother.

When sleep forsook my open eye,
Who was it sung sweet hushaby,
And rock'd me that I should not cry?
My Mother.

Who sat and watch's my infant head,
When sleeping on my cradle bed,
And tears of sweet affection shed?
My Mother.

When pains and sickness made me cry,
Who gaz'd upon my heavy eye,
And wept, for fear that I should die?
My Mother.

Who drest my doll in clothes so gay,
And taught me pretty how to play,
And minded all I had to say?
My Mother.

Who ran to me when I fell,
And would some pretty story tell,
Or kiss the place to make it well?
My Mother.

Who taught my infant lips to pray,
And love God's holy book and day?
And walk in wisdom's pleasant way?
My Mother...

III

SEASON OF CEREMONIES

[INSIDER WEEKLY, JUNE 17, 2002]

THE British Monarchy has remained prominently the reference point of public discourse in Britain since the Queen Mother, Elizabeth (1900-2002), passed on recently at the Windsor Castle. formerly, Elizabeth Bowes-Lyon, she was the wife of King George VI who ascended the British throne following the abdication of lover boy King Edward VIII, in 1936, to marry American divorcee, Wallis Simpson. To live for a whole century plus certainly gives cause for a celebration of life. You can therefore appreciate why Britons, in their thousands trooped out to pay a last homage to this matriarch of a sort, great grandmother. At Royal Holloway University of London, the principal, Professor Drummond Bone gave us permission on Tuesday, April 9 to observe a minute of silence in her honour. Those who were not satisfied with this simply went to join the long queue at Westminster Hall.

On April 15, I on my part went to Windsor, where I met a long queue of those waiting to catch a glimpse of the final resting place of the Queen Mother at the royal vault in St George Chapel but was not patient enough to wait, not with my weekly academic deadlines. The Archbishop of Canterbury, Dr. George Carey and poet laureate Andrew Motion took in much of the emotional outpouring. Archbishop Carey remarked that "we come to mourn but also to give thanks to celebrate the person and her life—both filled with such a rich sense of fun and joy and the music of laughter". In a long commemorative poem on the queen mother's centenary birthday anniversary, these prophetic lines were rendered by Motion:

Think of the flower lit coffin set
In vaulted public place, in state

So we who never knew you, but
all half suspect we knew you, wait,

and delve inside our heads, and find
the hash insistence in mind…

The departure from mother earth of the Queen Mother gave a fillip to the fading British royalty. From funeral to conviviality! Again, her daughter, Queen Elizabeth II, the reigning queen has just rounded off her golden jubilee—fifty years of her ascension to the throne—just before the mortal passage of her mother. She was guest to the British Parliament at Westminster Abbey not long ago. However, the main event of the anniversary reached a climax on 4th of June when she led a procession to St Paul's for a national thanksgiving service. Up to this point, it has been fun for Britain. At Newcastle-upon-Tyne, at the occasion of unveiling the statue of late Cardinal Basil Hume at St. Mary Cathedral, the Queen's entourage was greeted by Brynn Reed, 27, who was stark naked with "Rude Britannia" inscribed on his bottom. He ran alongside the Queen Rolls Royce and tried to press himself against the window. Anyway, Reed has since been charged with "outraging public decency". God knows what that is. Again, she will also mark her 76th birthday officially on June 15 though she was born on April 21, 1926. The British are in for a monarchical revival, notwithstanding that the monarchy now pays a symbolic income tax like every other citizen, thanks to the New Labour Parliament. I hope this wave of royal narcissism will not halt Labour's bid to turn Britain into a Republic. Afterall, Tony Blair is now been addressed as Head of State, thanks this time to Foreign Secretary, Jack Straw. Blair was in Texas ranch plotting with Bush how to overthrow Saddam Hussein when news of the Queen Mother's death was made Public. But as a commentator observed, the Monarchy is a symbol of continuity and unity of the nation enough, to talk less of its ossification. Let's wait and see.

I am not left out in these waves of celebration. I had just recently marked my 38th birthday, and this with profound merriment. Hitherto, I had always only taken stock of my annual cycle in poetic verses—without ceremony. The pull of my new environment with a bent for ceremonies was simply overwhelming. Thus, there was a gathering at my Highfield *en suite* apartment on Friday April 12. It was a medley of international students: Italians, Germans, Australians, Greece, Indians, Somalis, Ugandas, Zambians, Botswanans, Caribbeans, Kazakhstanis and British. It was a single humanity. There was no racial barrier as we chatted, danced and wined all the way. Politicians and Capitalists appeared to me the enemy of humanity. Politicians create artificial racial or ethnics bars to appropriate political power, and capitalists do the same for profit maximization. If power and capitalist motives are allowed to dominate world affairs as they appear to, a world without walls, hunger and diseases is doomed. Infact one of my many well-wishers said in a card sent to me: "with my utmost congratulations in turning thirty eight when life expectancy in Africa is thirty years." This statement to me reflected a deep appreciation of the global inequalities and the vertical relationship between the poor and rich countries of the world; a rat race in which everyone is on his /her mark, on the other hand, some are held back for others to go fast.

Back to me, with all the problems in Africa, which make her "the scar on the global conscience", one has every cause to be grateful to God. On another note, a friend here told me to be old is a state of the mind. Notwithstanding the truth in this assertion I am simply a realist, reasonable enough not to console myself with that sightless feminine obsession with external youthfulness. My cells are aging with each day that passes and it is this inner unseen dynamic that situates us on the journey from cradle to grave. The most important thing to me at the point I am on this journey is how much I could do to advance the cause of humanity before the embers flicker out. Forgive me, I can't help stating that at 38, I feel like Soyinka's Wasted Generation. Although, education is a lifelong affair, I am tagging along here in Britain with twenty-five year old men and women in a doctorate research. It is not funny and it is indeed a sad reminder of the wasted opportunities in my country; consequences of a tottering political order. In these parts of the world, at 38 you are already made, much of your contribution to humanity is already consummated. As Chief Obafemi of blessed memory always said the "past is always a story told why the future may be writ in gold".

Now, on May 29, the politicians in Abuja marked their third year in office with nothing to show for it in the main, and inspite of Obasanjo's obsession with re-writing our history June 12 remains sacrosanct and should stand as the nation's prime democracy day. Incidentally, my editor-chief at the *Insider Weekly* shares May 29 with the Abuja politicians' imposed democracy day as his birthday. He is simply ageless.

IV

MY EASTER TRIP TO THE NETHERLANDS

[INSIDER WEEKLY, APRIL 22, 2002]

CELEBRATING Easter in a foreign land without one's family, especially those of us in marital-hood could be lonely and nostalgic. This time I'm filled with memories of Easter with my family last year in Nigeria, driving all the way from Lagos to Benin, Warri, Ekpoma and Ososo and again back to Lagos in my old fashioned Swedish machine (Volvo). The only consolation is that this year's I 'm in the midst of relatives. My cousin in Landgraaf, Abraham Peter Evbota wanted me to chair his son's birthday and take a break from my academic work. So I obliged.

To get to Netherlands, I had to apply for a Schengen visa at the number 38 Hyde Park Gate office of the Dutch embassy in London. I made two abortive attempts to get the visa. Each time I was not early enough to beat the long queue. Since coming in from Egham, Surrey, where I am resident usually takes a while, I moved into London and stayed the night there and at 4.15 am on March 26, I was at the embassy by which time three others persons were already waiting. As it turned out, I was the fifth or so person on the queue and my application was approved. So, I picked up the visa on March 27.

Next the hassle of getting a flight from London to Maastricht in the Netherlands. All fights were fully booked for the Easter break. Thankfully, Priceline co.uk managed to book me a flight online from London Gatwick to Dusseldorf in Germany. On March 29 in Germany, I took the train to Aachen train station where my host, Abraham drove in across the German border to pick me up. Landgraaf is about twenty-five minutes drive across the German border.

And so, on March 30, I played the chair at the One Year Birthday of Bill Clinton Evbota, at Cafe Hofke Toon and Martha in the neighbourhood of Brunssum. Nigerians from all walks of life in the Netherlands and even from neighbouring Germany graced the occasion. My message to them was that they had to recognise the fact that the world is a theatre of struggle. Every stage one finds oneself at, one should know that it is a struggle; it is one of the principles of social Darwinism. This has been sunk into my brain by the radical literature I have read. Since coming into Britain September 2001, I have learnt the lesson of life everyday. It is a lesson in this logic that can make one George Bush and his errand companion, Tony Blair, to sit in Texas and decide that Saddam Hussein must go because they don't like his face. Anyway, as chair of the occasion, I was sensitive to alcohol and it paid off as I was drafted to take some of the guests home in the car as there were fewer hands to drive when the drinks went up the sleeve of so many a guest. Lest I forget, I was almost matched in an emergency marriage when a lady walked up to me and said: "look at your heights and a child by both of you could be something else." If I had concurred, likely my wife would be having a rival by now.

Much of my gusto was presently neutralised by Israel's atrocities in Palestine. Seeing the wreckage of Ramallah, and the demolition of Yasser Arafat's headquarters, you won't have to go far looking for the motivation of the suicide bombers. Suicide bombing becomes the last straw of a race battling for survival in its own land. This does not matter to the West, it is Saddam that matters; he is the threat to the peace of the Middle East. For those who know better, Saddam is the obstacle in the tunnel of oil-flow to the West, not the Sharons of this world. However,

I must say that there is a lot of solidarity among the British public to the cause of the Palestinians. But then again, it must be stressed that in this whole crisis, armed peace is no solution but genuine dialogue and mutual concession.

Beyond the Palestine tragedy, I arrived in London in the morning of April 3, and I was quite unsettled by a brief detention I was subjected to by a mean and overzealous lady who passed for a British immigration officer at the South Terminal of the Gatwick Airport.

Sometime ago, in March 1998 during our campaign against the Abacha regime, on my way from Germany barely a week after I had left Britain, I was to connect a flight, British Airways (BA) to Accra which was our window to the outside world in those dark days and wandered off to the North Terminal immigration control to inquire about how I could connect my flight on BA. My inquiry was turned into detention. At the end of my ordeal, my passport was stamped stating I had no transit visa. I was literally bundled into the BA flight which I had paid for legitimately to Accra. As soon as I arrived Lagos, I petitioned both the British High Commission and the consular head for record purposes.

So, as I handed over my passport to the lady in the morning of that day. She asked me if I had been denied entry into Britain before and I simply said yes in order to cut a long story short since my old passport had the "no transit" stamp of 1998. The wicked lady then filled my name on the "Home Office Form IS 18. Notice to a Person Required to Submit to Further Examination." After keeping me waiting for over forty minutes, she went inside an office, came back and told me it wouldn't happen again. I told her I felt embarrassed; that I was paying to study in Britain, not on charity. She took offence at that and took my passport asking me to apologise to her. Again, she wasted more of my time until I told her that I was sorry if she didn't like what I said. I hope the British authorities will find out who this lady is and do something about her insolence. As I said, the world is a turf of struggle, let us struggle to put our country right and avoid humiliating treatments such as the one I have just gone through.

V

WASHINGTON POST-INAUGURATION

[NATIONAL MIRROR, MARCH 11, 2009]

GOING to Washington after Obama's inauguration as the 44th President of the United States evoked all the excitement that would have gone with being around when the inauguration actually took place. I had wished winding back the hand of the clock just to be around on the day of inauguration and I really could have been there but in some way, I was not in full control of my trip; an organization was in charge and it determined at least when the consultation meeting on the Darfur crisis took place. I made it to Washington on January 29, some days after the inauguration. In the confines of my double-bed room at the prestigious and barely eight month old Gaylord National Resort and Convention Centre, I watched the television news and read the newspapers of the post-inauguration events and analysis.

The Gaylord Centre situated on the shores of the Potomac River in Washington, D. C, is symbolic of an aspect of the American dream—the grandiose. It is a place conceived to have everything under one roof: shopping mall, gymnasium, swimming pool and sundry conference and exhibition halls. To be sure, Gaylord Centre could host America in ways in which so many important national events can take place without any constituting an encumbrance to the other.

On a fleeting drive through Capitol Hill on my way to New York City by road, I realised that the hustle and bustle of Lagos, the commercial nerve centre and former capital of Nigeria was not in Political America; somewhat on the quiet side. However, the flurry of activities inside the White House was overwhelming as President Obama tried to settle into the business of governance. Putting a cabinet together was not all that smooth. His staunch supporter, Senator Tom Daschle, nominee for Health and Human Services, almost became his Achilles' heel. It elicited from the president on being elbowed by a foxy CNN's Anderson Cooper, the statement: 'I screwed up', that is, I made a mistake. Daschle had not paid $128,000 in taxes over three years. This obviously became an issue at the Senate confirmation; so electrifying that the Senator had to withdraw his candidacy. Timothy Geithner, Secretary of Treasury Department had similar problem in tax default but paid up with penalties. His was not as complicated as Daschle's. The conflicting figures made it worse. Watching Obama say, 'I screwed up,' and the corresponding response from viewers, I thought the president would have to be savvier in handling the press to avoid more such slips in the next four or eight years.

Swearing in of secretaries, an affair handled by the Vice President, Joe Biden highlighted in some emotional way the importance of family ties and value in the US. Former President Clinton and daughter stood by Hillary when she took the oath of office as Secretary of State. The threesome held themselves as in a congregational prayer. It evinced love and perhaps bond in the family.

In down town Washington, the new first lady, Michelle and the wife of the Vice President, Jill Biden, were seen playing guest to several important people and places. Adrian Fenty, Mayor of Washington DC was found to have had the honour of playing host to the first lady and Jill at Georgia Brown's restaurant, enough to attract camera calls. As this was going on, a bit of the Obama effect was demonstrated in the election of Michael Steele as Republican National Committee Chairman. It is hoped that Steele's magic will revamp the GOP as he promised. All these constituted an additional accomplishment to my main reason for the trip.

The downside of my stay in Washington however is that I starved due to the availability of only fast foods (take this as a metaphor for non-African food at least at the Gaylord Centre). Frankly speaking this was not a good bargain for a man that is used to swallow: *eba* and pounded yam and other soup-accompanying foods. So I craved for Nigerian-like cuisine. Prof. Bolaji Aluko of Howard University came to the rescue when he took us (Ola Soyinka, Felix Oriakhi of Benson Idahosa University and my humble self) to the National Church, Fort Washington, where a Nigerian woman, Princess Abigail Bola Babalola, was celebrating her birthday. We joined the convivial crowd, definitely not as interlopers, and helped ourselves to Fried Rice cum Jolof Rice with plantain and meat. That was on the eve of our departure from Washington DC—and what a parting menu.

Nevertheless, more important issues besetting the America state as the Obama administration commences, takes over my thoughts, among the state of the America economy; in the midst of job losses in America, one could not help wondering what could happen to a relative of mine in Heywood, California with the daily news of lay-offs in American companies and corporations. May be Obama's stimulus plan, which seems anchored on economic nationalism would reverse the trend. We hope.

VI

MANY WISHES OF XMAS AND NEW YEAR

[DECEMBER 2008]

THE belief in Almighty God humbles us in more ways than one. We also believe that we are subject to supernatural forces that shape our earthly destinies irrespective of our will. Many of us believe that we can access God through prayers and other forms of penitence and submission and attain corresponding divine blessings in whatever form; the practice of which has assumed a mystique of sorts. Conventionally, we use festive periods to dramatise the faith.

Last festive period, I felt humbled by the many wishes I received. One of the text messages read, "favour is d flavour dat adds colour 2 man's labour, a day of favour is more than a lifetime of labour. May God dazzle you wit his favour dis Xmas and New Year season". Another well-wisher wrote, "'these are the hands that God will bless.' May the spirit of joy & the blessing of peace be yours at Christmas. May God stay beside you & those you love throughout the New Year." Of interest is this one which ran with poetic cadence: "when grace is @ work, natural laws ar' put on hold, protocols are suspended, formalities are waved. His dear grace will speak 4 u dis Xmas and in year 2009 in Jesus name." One well-wisher sent his payers in a loaded car visually represented and the note read, "the car is loaded with blessings, joy, peace, happiness, success, good health etc. Off load it, it's all urs dis xmas season." What follows came from yet another Well-wisher: "May d doors of unspeakable joy be open to u and every member of ur family dis yuletide and may the new yr present u d best of life's gifts. The next one came from a pastor. I was awed by the lines which ran thus: "Watch what u THINK&/or ASK this 2009, becos God wl superabundantly surpass all ur THINKING +ASKINGS in Jesus Name! (Emphasis in original)." The one that followed also came in a prophetic tone: "In 2009, I prophesy 4 u & ur fmly greatnes unequald, favour unlimited & mercy inexhaustbl, no mtr d circumstances, d cnspracs of forces of darkness & d wickd plans of all enems cmbined, God wl surely elevate you even abv dm all. God will establsh u & do what no man can do IJN, amn."

Indeed, before the next text message came urging me to claim them, I had claimed every prayer and wish with a loud amen in a bit of monologue. "Claim it now," the message began, "where the eagles fear, u will dare. Where others fail, u will succeed. D sky shall be ur springboard & d Lord shall be ur strength." Although Friedrich Nietzsche claimed that "it is a subtle point that God learned Greek when he decided to become a writer—and that he did not learn it better." My well-wishers wrote in English and had adapted it in ways well beyond the imagination of the Englishman.

Truly, some of the messages were also political. One read: "as the ruling class and the elite wish each other a prosperous new year don't forget the majority of our people who never had prosperity when oil sold at $147 per barrel. Can 2009 be prosperous with oil at $40? Another wished that "2009 will be just fine for you & yours, & that in 2009 our country will bcom one where justice & peace provide foundation 4 progress & prosperity."

The wishes and prayers traversed the endless fields of idealism and realism; idealism—the belief in what otherworldliness can offer and realism—the affirmation of the objective reality of our world. Thus, where idealism ends, rationalism takes over. To pursue the point of those who ventured into the political grounds with the thrust of their messages, I would say that the development of our country hangs precariously on the fortune of oil. The prevailing blues in the oil sector could mean a halt to capital project. The ill-advised devaluation of the naira could also stymie the real sector. As a consequence, state actors would for sure resort to fresh loans and negate whatever good there is in the so-called exit from the Paris club. And back to idealism, let me end with this prayer which also came into my message pool. "Take the new yr as ur own 2 shape according 2 ur dreams. May happiness b truly urs".

VII

CHISTMAS WITHOUT PONMO

[PREMIUM TIMES ONLINE, DECEMBER 25, 2015]

TODAY is Christmas. The big question is how many Nigerians can really merry and embrace in merriment, a season's embrace wrapped with peals of laughter. Given the palpable suffering of most of the population in long-lasting struggle to eke out a living and its compounding by a bunch of reckless state actors, the hilarity of Christmas is at least gone for today. In pains, the suffering masses would continue their existential drudgery in search of what to eat. This undermines hope, a panacea of sorts. From the beginning of the year, in their toil for what to eat, a hardly fruitful endeavour in this clime, hope is always there like a shadow trailing its owner.

Christmas is a season for new clothes, eating and wining. Some culinary finesse is brought to bear on our diet. Beef, chicken, fish, crayfish, prawns and *ponmon*. The latter is known by many names such as *kanda* and *ohian*. Its value lies in being affordable and also mouthful. Medicine men says it's cholesterol full, others say it is wholesome for the liver, yet there is the view that it has no nutritious value. Also, an indolent ruling class is even considering tapping into an estimated 75 billion dollar global leather industry where cow skin or *ponmo* ought to be. Fears of chemicals and contamination are even being invoked to dissuade the poor from his/her preference. Whatever the views, they are the reason while it is the refuge of the poor and always tops a sense of a wholesome meal. It is an easy complement in the combination called in the South-West, orisiorisi (assorted meat).

Irrespective of their faiths, poor Nigerians often look forward to Christmas; not really for its religious essence but for the leisure it offers, the vent its provides for a momentary mirth of life in which we are at one with the creator; inspired by his work of creation, we would exclaim: life is beautiful! Today, hope is driven away, or shall we say smashed, not a lick of the lips and the crunching of *ponmon*, the choice of the impoverished Nigerians, which by some ironic and weird force of attraction is also patronised by those responsible for their misery.

In spite of the masses' impoverishment, already hemmed in the margins of bare existence and uncertainty of a season, our tomorrow, if there may be one is already being overshadowed by our tormentors, mouthpieces of IMIFI JUJU, known as Bretton Woods institutions, and a man who promised 'change' is telling them to prepare for pains over obvious economic downturn that they did not engender, others demented are clamouring for the removal of oil subsidy, an imaginary specie, you and I know, does not exist but a fraudulent carbuncle inflicted on the people by the thieving elite. Others are projecting tolls for unpassable roads while the naira is racing towards Golgotha. Agencies that provide power and energy have upped their tariff blatantly without improvement on their services.

Aforesaid, hope is a panacea. Where is hope? It is being attacked by our tormentors in ways that made good old John Keats say that pains abide forever with us while happiness is a rare visitor. As Shakespeare's Cassius in Julius Caesar puts it, oppressed people when burdened never lack the means to dismiss the fetters of oppression. In his words,

> *...Cassius from bondage will deliver Cassius: Therein, ye gods, you make the weak most strong; Therein, ye gods, you tyrants do defeat: Nor stony tower, nor walls of beaten brass, Nor airless dungeon, nor strong links of iron, Can be retentive to the strength*

of spirit; But life, being weary of these worldly bars,
Never lacks the power to dismiss itself. If I know this,
know all the world besides, That part of tyranny, that
I do bear, I can shake off at pleasure.

Cassius envisages suicide or revolt. The option for our people maybe the latter. The toiling people of this country would perhaps invoke the general will to damn their traducers and oppressors. This could take on different social expressions. The country is already contending with Boko Haram insurgents in the North-East, Indigenous People of Biafra, Niger-Delta militants, one of the most impoverished enclave in the world, Odua revivalism is lurking at the corner and who knows, very soon, Ogiso brigade would emerge from the Mid-West. These processes are irreversible for a people beaten to the wall. History is there for us. The Americans took on the British tax masters in 1760s, the Cuban people triumphed over Batista and his gangs in 1959 and the Bolsheviks took on the reactionary forces and the Czar scums in Russia in 1917.

The suffering of our people today reminds me of the signature tune of Hotel de Jordan, a drama series in Nigeria Television Authority (NTA) Benin, written and produced by the inimitable Comrade Jonathan Ihonde, in the early seventies which goes as follows: "God save us make we no see trouble; who see one no dey know whether na white or yellow; poor man dey suffer, monkey dey work, baboon dey chop". As toiling Nigerians cannot merry today, eat their ponmo, let it be known that their days of 'suffering and smiling' will be over (apologies to Fela Anikulapo-Kuti). They shall claim their day, they shall have their laugh, and they shall merry again with shouts of victory over their oppressors.

VIII

IS THIS VIRUS DEADLIER THAN AIDS?

[INSIDER WEEKLY. FEBRUARY 11, 2002]

DEAR reader, let me quickly introduce myself as an off shore member of the *Insider Weekly* family. As the scribe of some of the major prodemocracy groups in the country in the Babangida and Abacha years, I was the main advocate of the *Idobolo* philosophy, i.e., "mounting of the barricades" against the military and this would include the current interim political compromise which is not free from the ethos of the military; it needs to be nurtured into full democratic recovery. These are times that call for the battle of the mind as well as of the street when occasion demands and this is precisely what yours sincerely will be doing from my Egham base in the United Kingdom, where I am currently undergoing purification in a scholastic monastery. The battle menu I shall be serving you weekly will be both political and mundane, a mix bag of political issues and existential by-ways from across the world.

Let me start by announcing that winter virus is here in the United Kingdom. At first I thought it was just the freezing winter cold which I dread and had readied myself for. The trick is wearing as many as four clothes which makes me look like an Igbo masquerade. In addition, I occasionally take a glass of beer to keep my intestines warm. The virus blowing across the UK from Manchester to Glasgow is to my knowledge yet to reach Egham. If it comes, yours sincerely might not be spared from it except by the special grace of the immunity I have built up from eating starch—I mean *eba, amala* and *akpu (santana)* over the years. You could become a victim of this virus if you are within three metres of an infected person, so says Dr. Philip Marks. It is very contagious and spreads very easily. It does not respond to all disinfectants except bleach-based ones. A victim often exhibits the following symptoms: lack of energy, vomiting and fatigue. However, it is not as deadly as the almighty AIDS and you do not need to worry about a routine with the expensive cocktail and the prospect of the exploitative West not allowing a Thabo Mbeki to massify the cocktail for the benefit of hapless victims. This is currently the scourge of the people in the aforementioned British cities. Pray it doesn't reach an emergency level such that yours sincerely will have to flee the monastery for the safe haven of winter-free Lagos, the city of excellence.

IX

SEX AND SOCCER

[INSIDER WEEKLY, JULY 29, 2002]

ORDINARILY, I am not given in to football. I

lost interest in it since 1986 when General Babangida introduced quota system into a game that is essentially about skill. He did not only stop at that, he began to use the game's popularity in the country as a means of diversion from his regime's bad policies, especially the structural adjustment programme (SAP) and gross human rights violation. When the last edition of world cup—Korea/Japan 2002—began, I did not bother to watch the matches. I knew that the presence of Nigeria at the mundial would be short lived. You cannot expect to make a headway with a team that is a product of politics. As it turned out, the team crashed out from the tournament. However, I somehow ended momentarily my self-imposed disinterestedness about soccer because of my current host country, Britain, whose citizens are football fanatics. I basked with them in the euphoria of England winning the cup. So, I watched England tie with Brazil as well as the grand finale: Brazil vs. Germany. I think the Samba Boys played scientific football and the better side won.

Interestingly, this time football commentaries in the British media had an erotic angle with it. *News of the World,* which claims to be the official world cup newspaper, heralded the world cup contest with an eight-page pull out of gorgeous and sizzling babes in their most sensuous forms—semi-nude and sturdy with scintillating bursts and hypnotic bottom. Before this debut, it was in the news that the English coach, Mr. Sven-Goran Eriksson was hit by a thunder bolt in the tasty Swedish blonde, Ulrika Jonsson to the discomfiture of his old heart throb, Nancy Dell'Olio. As soon as England crashed out of the mundial. Some British television beamed out footages of Eriksson's sizzling affairs. Eriksson was made to face the two apples of his eye and I guess his answer would have been interesting had he been asked the Freudian question: what is on a man's mind? English player, Gareth Southgate, promised to marry his fiancée, Brazilian Paula McGrory, 26, if England won the world cup. I hope the centre will still hold for them now that England did not make it. Gareth was however so sure whatever the turn of event, altar they go.

Again, England's encounter with Brazil was heralded by *The Sun* with the 23 year old blonde Lisa Collins' claims of a marathon sex encounter with the Brazilian whiz-kid, Ronaldinho in a hotel in Paris. The Ex-Manchester shop girl, Lisa enthused with vivid reminiscences: "the greatest night that I could have wished for….I have never had so much pleasure… I must admit that Ronaldinho was not the best looking man I have been with. But he more than made for that with the sensuous touch—not just with his hands …After an hour we laid back on the king side bed both satisfied." Ronaldinho was to demonstrate his bed skills in the turf with a freakish goal, which sent everybody, including David Seaman, the English Goalkeeper, gazing at nowhere in particular until the net shook unbelievably with the ball.

As Brazil made a triumphant entry into the final, its coach Mr. Phil Scolari had become impatient. His mind was set on one thing: sex with his wife. His abstention in the course of the soccer battle made him so much impatient that he needed a break. Hear him: "Of course we want to win the world cup—that is why we are here. But I am looking forward to at least seven days away from all this so that I can sleep with my wife." His wife is very lucky, with a mind filled with joy of victory, Phil's bed session with his wife is best imagined.

Abstention was however not in the lexicon of the Senegalese. Reports had it that the Senegalese mingled football with emotion as their lovers were tied to their boot–laces, and at some point they had to abandon work-outs. Could this be responsible for their lack-luster outing against the Turks?

While his countrymen were relishing the excitement of the world cup back home in Japan, Kenici Aoyama was busy taking photographs of women's knickers in shops with a camera hidden under a newspaper. He also took photographs of his unsuspecting victims' faces to match their Knickers. Aoyama reveled in this "up skirting" past time for about four months taking snapshots in Harolds, W.H Smith and Boots until he was caught by the long arm of the law, Aoyama, a student at Oxford University who built an album of about 2400 photos of his victims had been sentenced to a three-month imprisonment by District Judge Simon Cooper of West London Magistrate Court. He is to be deported afterwards. Hmm! Soccer and Sex.

X

THE DRESS CODE OF A SOCIALIST

[THE GUARDIAN, APRIL 10, 2013]

I write this piece in honour of Deacon Ayo Ositelu. He was my senior colleague in *The Guardian* Editorial Board. He joined his ancestors last January. God bless his soul! I was unable to pay my last respect to this veteran sports analyst and prolific writer as I had travelled to the United Kingdom to deliver some lectures earlier scheduled before Ayo's home call; two of them at Royal Holloway and School of Oriental and African Studies (SOAS), both colleges of the University of London and the third on the platform of Leadership Society of Nigeria (LSN) was delivered in South East London. In those lectures I reflected on issues bordering on the dynamics of Nigerian politics and development.

Ayo was a great Nigerian and numerous individuals who paid tribute to him testified to his greatness. Our country is blessed with so many great people, yet, they have been rendered irrelevant by a warped, self-serving and disoriented leadership endowed with what Paulo Freire calls magical consciousness or semi-intransitive consciousness which is characterised by limited perception and the inability to comprehend causality.

Social relations, for me, constitute the basis of reminiscence and appreciation of the worth of a fellow human being. The last conversation between Ayo and I was memorable. He often sat in opposite direction to my seat, so we began our exchange through notes in order not to disturb the trend of debate at the board. I told him that I was going to make it the kernel of an opinion article. The subject was the type of clothes I wear and by extension a critical question of what socialists, pseudo or genuine should wear. Our discussion went thus: "those who suspect that the notable 'socialist' (your good self) has turned 'capitalist', may have a weapon to argue their case, when they notice the quality of the 'safari' suits you wear these days," Deacon wrote. "The concept of safari suit is not one of cut-and-nail but one with aesthetics and perimeters," I replied. Lest I forget, the concept of 'safari' suits is one thing; the evident quality (Italian cut) is another. No offence," he wrote again. This was to be the last of such an exchange. Ayo was soon to bid us all goodbye.

Going back in time, I remember confronting this question about how a socialist should dress in the early 1990s and as an undergraduate of the University of Lagos. As a leading member of the Marxist-Leninist Study Group (MLSG), I caused a meeting to hold at the Arts Block of the University where the matter was thoroughly debated. The summary of the proceedings at that conference was that comrades who could afford good clothes should wear them.

What is not in doubt is that the 'elected ancestors' of our ideology, Marx, Engels and Lenin wore excellent suits. Looking further into history, comrades in other climes who waged guerrilla wars against the state could not have become ceremonial fops. Fidel Castro and company could not have been so in the mountains of the Sierra Mastra. There was no way Che Guevara could have become groovy in the woods of Bolivia. Amilcar Cabral could not have become one in the swamps of Guinea Bissau. Dressing is a product of people's culture and arises from the transformation of productive forces. Also, style and texture are conditioned by climatic conditions and other considerations.

To be a socialist or partisan of the working class could be determined by a number of criteria. A primary criterion is class belongation determined by the position one occupies in the production relations. You either sell your labour to eke out a living or own the means of production and therefore an employer of labour. The second criterion is class consciousness, which leads one always to take side with the exploited class in society. And thirdly, class actions, demonstrable in the practical activities that are redemptive of the oppressed in society. Class solidarity may prevent many socialists who have the means to buy fine clothes to remain untailored.

The magical consciousness, which the ruling clique in our country has imposed on society today, is that the oppressed people tend to see their future in the consumerist image of the oppressors who don on large flowing *Agbada*, expensive suits and cruise about in bullet-proof and siren-equipped cars. The ruled now equate anything less with poverty without seeing them as the foundation of the erosion of the distributive and social values in society.

Deacon Ositelu was not a professed socialist but he lived such a simple life that it put him on the same social spectrum with the toiling masses of our people. Today, there is quite a number of comedians in government hoodwinking the masses of our people by their socialist claims. As Chief Awolowo always said, the past is always a story told while the future may be writ in gold. I, for sure, dream of a society where all Nigerians can live well and dress well, not a differentiated one with ghettos and highbrow quarters.

XI

CUBAN NOTES

[THE GUARDIAN, JULY 14, 2013]

YOU left Lagos on an evening flight aboard Air France on the way to Cuba via Paris and you were overwhelmed by a riot of imagination of what to expect in the Caribbean island. Would you see Papa Fidel? Would you see the remains of the guerrilla sculptor, Ernesto Che Guevara and Camilo Cienfuegos? Would you see a new society free from the exploitative relations of a pseudo-capitalist society? Would you see a workers society? How about your kinsfolk born of ancestors who were shipped in the days of yore to work in the sugar and cotton plantations of the Americas as slaves? Would you see them truly free? Would you be free to embrace the "winning carriage, skin tone and beauty" of the island, on an even keel, without the exchange of filthy lucre? What merchandise would be available in the malls to shop from? You stretched your imagination almost limitlessly.

After the second leg of a long flight from Paris to Havana you then arrived at Jose Marti International Airport without the allure of Heathrow in London or JFK in New York. You sought the razzmatazz of the fabled socialist republic. The immigrations officials appeared overwhelmed by a stream of tourists fascinated by the tropical weather of the island while fleeing from the deadly winters of the Alps and meadows of Europe. You could imagine that these visitors were a mix of genuine tourists and sprinkling of agents of Uncle Sam. For sure, the agents would not escape the data capturing tools of the dutiful Cuban immigration officers who fed into their data bank detail of every alien on the soil of the Bayamese. You would not lose the sense of order, which the immigration officials brought to bear on the process of clearing the mammoth crowd of visitors. You noticed that they performed their duty, in a manner of speaking, with revolutionary precision.

Jetlagged, you were transported to your hotel room, Hotel Presidente, somewhere in New Havana. You noticed that all through the short journey to the hotel, there were no potholes on the well-paved highway and streets and no traffic gridlock. As you settled into your room on the fifth floor, you took an aerial view of Havana—old and new—a lovely tropical city on the Atlantic waters with skyscrapers. You passed them for five star hotels back home. You were wrong; they were all dwellings for the Cuban people. You inquired who planned this city and were told, not to mind, it was modeled in every way after Miami.

The jetlag was soothed by a night rest despite the difference in time zone, to which you would later adjust. On your day one you ventured into the city and you got the shocker of your life. You could hardly see the picture of the revolutionary legend, Fidel, adorning the streets of Cuba conspicuous only in the Revolutionary Square, a pantheon that hosted the portraits of Che, Fidel Ruz Castro, Eduardo de Santos and Hugo Chavez. As a friend of the Cuban people, you visited Amistur for a brief tutorial on civics regarding the country of Immanuel Cespedes. The building, which housed Amistur had before the revolution belonged to a latifundia owner who forfeited it to the workers state. The next day you travelled to Santa Clara, the city, which had chosen Che as their son. You encountered all the relics of his eventful revolutionary life in a massive Museum. At Santa Clara, you were amazed at the adoration of Che. His statue with his famous fatigue, haversack and a rifle announced the museum and some kilometres apart you came across the armoured train with which Che joined the battle against the Batista regime. As his son, Camilo Guevara observed in his preface to *The Bolivian Diary*, "Against their will, Che is transformed into a hardened symbol of resistance, a symbol of the fight for what is just, of passion, of the necessity of being fully human, multiplied infinitely in the ideals and weapons of those who struggle. This is what the front men and their omnipotent handlers fear."

With the US blockade, described by Gabriel Garcia Marquez, the Nobel laureate and author of *One Hundred Years of Solitude*, as one of the worst human right violations of the 20th century, you wondered how the small island country had managed to survive. You were goaded to traverse Matanzas province, another wonder. Matanzas did appear as the food basket of the country. No wonder Freer Bridget wrote in Marie Claire a few years ago that for Cuba the future was orange. "Struggling Cubans would survive," you blurted out in unveiled solidarity with the beleaguered children of Marti and Antonio Maceo.

If Matanzas was a spectacle, the May Day event was even more amazing, with leftists from the whole of Latin America and elsewhere in the world gathered in Havana to mark the workers day. You were driven to the revolutionary square to observe the parade as early as 4 am in the morning so that you would be able to stay at a vantage position to watch the events. May Day, was an all-city affair, everyone, old and young, including the military took part in the parade unarmed. You observed that it was the height of workers solidarity, a 'force for itself', ready to defend the revolution and simultaneously it dawned on you where the strength of the revolution laid. Since January 1959 when the July 26 Movement triumphed over Batista's dictatorship, Cuba had retained its revolutionary mystique. You learnt that on the same May Day, in Seattle, USA, workers' rights of association and expression were rudely assaulted by the police and that many peaceful protesters were wounded. You thought it ironic for a society that laid claim to being a land of freedom. What a contrast!

You would not be fair to your readers if you did not share a view on the organization of the Cuban economy, which ran on the wheels of tourism. The tourist economy was anchored on the icons of the revolution. Sculptures, T-shirts, and hats with Jose Marti, Fidel, Che or Cienfuegos as the central motifs adorned the shopping centres. Soyinka observed in his *Ibadan, The Pekelemes Years* the dominance of Fidel in everything but with a caveat that, "the personality cult was not contrived, it was not a phenomenon that was carefully nurtured. Cuba's personality cult was very simply the force of Fidel Castro — his history, personality, will-power and oratorical intensity." Over half a century of the revolution, you reasoned that the personality cult was not a cult but the history of the Cuban people, a history that transcended Fidel and embraced his comrades in arms and their forebears who built the Cuban history of resistance.

Lonely in the confines of your hotel room, you sauntered into the cold airy Havana night; you encountered beautiful women with whom you made friends. You found the women submissive, friendly and somewhat untamed by the revolution. You looked at these beautiful humans; the mulattoes and your transformed kindred snatched from Africa some five hundred years ago, these were a perfect sort. If Havana women were beautiful, what of the women of the Oriente province for whom Soyinka waxed lyrical. In his *Ibadan, The Pekelemes Years,* he captured insightfully aspects of the post-liberation Cuban society of the 1960s. He pointed out an emerging trend of the revolution. Truly, the overthrown Batista government had regimented social life in Cuba, but a regimentation of thoughts was emerging "as the 'second' revolution—the Marxist one—fastened its hold on the society." Even then he noted the laissez faire life in the Oriente province, especially Santiago de Cuba, 'where the people walked and talked like thinking, not programmed, beings. The daily sociology of the Oriente was loose-limbed, spontaneous, and independent, a marked contrast to Habana." "And the women of the Oriente had a winning carriage, skin tone and beauty," that in a choice of place for exile, for him, it would be Santiago de Cuba, "or nowhere else on earth!" Quite frankly, a narrative of Cuba would be incomplete without an account of the daily rhythm of life at the margins, aspects of which Julio Travieso Serrano accounted for in *Raining Over Havana.*

Seeing the modest achievement of the revolution, you wondered how Cuba managed to survive thus far in the belly of the beast; a beast roaring with the anger of a wounded lion. You recalled that on the eve of the revolution, Uncle Sam was Cuba's biggest trading partner, accounting for about 60-70 percent of the country's exports and import. The US relied on Cuban sugar and tobacco. But the Agrarian Reform law of the revolution marked the parting of ways. The revolution expropriated the expropriators to aggrandize landless farm families. For a country that had made Cuba a new colony of sorts through the Platt Amendment that emasculated Cuba's sovereignty, it was too much to bear. Between 1959 and 1964, the US leadership imposed a crippling and seemingly eternal economic blockade on the country. Fidel had retorted that "The people of Cuba will have to love their revolution more, because every new obstacle that's placed in our path will mean that we'll have to fight harder and make more sacrifices for it." The following thoughts ran in your mind: "Cubans really are paying a price for independence:

empty malls, old cars and horse drawn carts and hurricane-beaten homes in old Havana that reminded you of Isale Eko. Despite the insufficiency, the wheel of Cuba runs. Out of hardship, it has emerged a world health power despite emigration to the US of over 50 percent of its medical doctors shortly after the revolution. Medicare is free for her people and so is education. The state provides jobs but not to satisfy the appetite of the petit bourgeois brats. With the blockade, Cuba would have been a realization of Robert Owens failed Utopia—a workers commune."

Beyond the ideology that underpinned the revolutionary society, you ran into a horde of Osun state delegates in the cities of Cuba; you became curious as to their mission— a brigade of youths of the Osun Youth Empowerment Scheme who did voluntary agro work in Cuban farms and had a feel of the Cuban biotech in company of volunteers from over 50 countries. They were at the May Day parade in Havana. You remembered that Cuba is home to Yoruba culture. Yamaya (Yemoja) was well-regarded and both Havana and Matanzas harboured Yoruba cultural relics and deities. Truly, you saw the Cuban *Babalawos* wore hand beads. The helmsman at Osun, Ipinle Omoluabi, was enamoured of the Cuban example of a welfare state. The state must feed itself; the population must be educated with meals-on-wheel for primary school pupils and *Opon Imo* for secondary school students.

Home-bound, you had regrets you could not visit Santiago de Cuba and have a view of the Moncada Barracks which youthful Fidel and a band of volunteers attacked in the run-up to the struggles that wrought the Cuban revolution. You missed out on Varadero beach, one of the showpieces of the Cuban tourist industry, despite your journey through the Matanzas province.

Your mind raced to the waiting nightmare of Charles De Gaulle Airport in Paris for the Lagos-bound journey and the Cuban reverie were taken over by the Nigerian blues—Boko Haram, kidnappers, power outage, government by committees and so on.

XII

CHE GUEVARA: TWENTY-EIGHT YEARS AFTER THE MORTAL OCTOBER

[THE GUARDIAN, OCTOBER 17, 1988]

NO one can be more deserving of a tribute than a man who devoted his entire life to the service of humanity and like the Biblical Christ died for humanity. That man was Ernesto Che Guevara de La Serna.

This month the world remembers the heroic guerrilla who blew cold wind into intelligence circles and made reactionary regimes the world over to sit up and be alert.

Ernesto Che Guevara was born in 1928 in the River Plate area of Argentina, South America. But then, no one could gaze at the crystal-ball and say young "Che" would lift the banner of freedom for the oppressed all over the world.

Che Guevara was an engineer, a doctor, economist, politician, army commander, photographer, revolutionary and writer. This fact made Jean Paul Sartre to describe him as "the most complete man of his time a man distinguished by the stupendous many sidedness of his personality."

Che Guevara, the Gaucho, grasped early the reality of the social miseries of Argentina. His family was democratic and allowed "Che" to mix with the poor, eat their meal and drink their brew. According to Isabel Larguia, the Argentinean essayist "it was with them that he learned the ABCs of misery and vulnerability". His father was equally part of his creation. Don Ernesto Guevara Lynch who had written a book on his son entitled *My Son Che* told the Cuban Weekly, *Bohemic* before his mortal passage on April 1, 1987, at the age of 87, that he was instrumental to the making of Che. "I was the one who put those ideas into his head," he said.

Today, there are two main media of expressing thoughts, ideas and experiences, one is utterance the other, writing. As

Che Guevara began his peregrinations through Latin America in his deepest craving to grasp the essence of social miseries in that part of the world, he realised that his experience had to be registered in writing if the scientific truth must be told. In the words of Thomas Hobbes "words are wise men counters, they do but reckon by them". So Che did.

His journeys now described as pilgrimages, saw him through, among other countries, Chile, Venezuela, Guatemala, Peru and Colombia. In Valparaiso, Chile he wrote in his diary to register the human lot: "The poor were pitiful, their hovels reeked of the rancid odour of concentrated sweat and dirty feet mixed with dusty rockers, the only furniture they had. Asthma and heart disease were rampant. That is when a doctor, who realises his helplessness, wants change, and end to injustice which up until a month ago had that poor old woman working as assistant to earn her living, exhausted and suffering but facing life with an upright attitude…There in the last moments of those whose farthest horizon was always the next day is where you see the deep tragedy of lives of the world proletariat." Also in Chuquimata, he observed in his diary the miseries of a working-class couple whose lot is symbolic of the workers the world over.

Che's letter to his father which subject was the Lima Asylum captures his essence, sincerity and devotion as revolutionary to the service of humanity. He wrote: "They were friendly to us because we did not wear dust shields or gloves and shook hands with them as if they were the neighbours' son and sat to chat with them about anything and everything…It may seem a pointless risk but the psychic good it did those sick who are treated like savage beasts, the mere fact they were regarded like normal being is invaluable…" Those jottings perhaps were the cradle of the writer in him

His on-the-spot assessment of the ordinary run of mankind in Latin America launched him on a historic mission. As he observed, he "had been tossed by the social waves convulsing Latin America". The Cuban revolution of 1959 became the pilot scheme to crystallize his dream of an international freedom for the oppressed. He moved from one theatre of liberation struggling to another in Vietnam, Algeria, Zaire and Bolivia. He met his death in Bolivia on October 8, 1967 in the hands of Bolivia troops and CIA operatives.

His poem: "Song to Fidel" demonstrated his allegiance and dedication to the cause of Cuban revolution.

> *Let's go ardent prophet of the dawn by secret unbarbeb paths to liberate the green crocodile you love so much.*
>
> *Let's go avenging outrage with our foreheads full of Marti's rebel stars we swear to be victorious or to die when the first shots ring out and awaken the entire forest in virgin surprise there at your side will be us the fighters you will have us…*

His revolutionary thoughts and ideas as practiced by him found expression in his works. Among his works are *Socialism and man in Cuba, Venceremos*, a collection of his writings; *Classics of Guerrilla Warfare*, and *Che Speaks*, a collection of his interviews. These works remain his greatest legacy to mankind.

There is no other accolade to describe "Che Guevara" than what Nicolas Guillen, Cuban National poet wrote in his poem, *Che Commandante*:

> *Not because you have fallen is your light less high.*
> *A horse of fire sustains you, guerrilla sculpture between*
> *the winds and the clouds of the Sierra…*

I conclude in the words of Fidel Castro, let us be like Che.

XIII

BLOODBATH AT BAYERO

[THE GUARDIAN, FEBRUARY 21, 1993]

PENULTIMATE Friday while politicians were scheming and contriving poll winning strategies all over the country, Nigerian students' delegates were milling into Bayero University Kano (BUK) for their scheduled 11th convention of the National Association of Nigerian Student (NANS). It was an occasion when a new executive council of the students' umbrella organisation was to be elected to pilot affairs for the new academic session.

Before their arrival, the delegates had had high hopes and expectations for exciting and fun-filled event. There was also the attraction of the ancient city of Kano once famed for its hides and skin, and its ancient walls. Nothing betrayed the bloody commotion that would ensue later excepting the windy and chilly atmosphere which occasioned by the harmattan was not unusual. The peaceful atmosphere was palpable and infectious. Delegates hugged one another while echoing intermittently their solidarity calls: *A luta continua, vitória é certa*.

Shortly before nightfall, a rally in line with the event's programme, was summoned by the executive council of the local students' union at the instance of the delegates. A crowd gathered and those billed to make speeches mounted the rostrum. Each of them delivered a message to the teeming audience. Their messages focused essentially on the heroic exploits of Nigerian students dating back to early 1940s. There was, however, a notable unusual but similar thread that also ran through all the speeches; each speaker sought to distance and divest the convention of any religious coloration. It was stressed that the convention was a forum for debating the common lot of Nigerian students with special regard to education and the polity.

The concerted efforts made to distance religion from the purpose of the convention should have been a warning signal to the general delegates that there was a fragile calm on the campus. As the irresistible hands of night held sway over the fast receding sunlight, some delegates had to find their way back to the hostels, clean up and relax while others stood in groups chatting away, drinking (non-alcoholic beverages), smoking cigarettes or just sauntering about. There was no light; power had been cut to make matters worse, so also was water and these, as soon as the delegates arrived, we were told. But nature in its strange logic came to the rescue as the moon which had turned full circle blazed on in the night.

It was at this point that some religious fanatics among the BUK students known variously, as UMMA, USTAZ and Mullahs appeared and started attacking the students' delegates and the press corp. First they went to Idris Garba Hall, rapped menacingly on the door of the student activists and union officials. In some cases they forced doors open and searched for delegates. The attack was carried out with occasional shouts of *Allah Akbar* (Allah is great) renting the air. Delegates started running for dear life. There was pandemonium everywhere punctuated by shrill cries of people in agony. The campus soon appeared like a ghost town.

The NANS leadership mustered its constituency and solidarity songs to surmount the eerie calm and solitude. Those who had fled in the wake of the attack emerged from their hide-outs. Some had cuts in the hands, legs, and with bruises all over their bodies. They bled. But it was not yet over.

A second attack followed. The mullahs who had tactically retreated before the re-emerging crowd of students regrouped and attacked the defenseless delegates, this time, with more gusto. Like the previous attack, there was panic. Delegates and pressmen ran berserk and without bearing into the endless stretch of desert. They had to stay awake in the open desert in the freezing cold. This writer was not left out. Even students of BUK who hail from the south sought refuge in the little cover that the Sahel vegetation could offer. The following day when delegate came back from their hideouts, there was a heated debate and it bordered on whether the convention could still hold at BUK or not. It was then that the Mullahs launched yet another attack which was to be the last. They came in fifteen fully loaded buses which had been hijacked from the Edo State University delegates. Armed with highly lethal weapons, they attacked the unsuspecting delegates who had thought that their fellow comrades had arrived in the buses. This time, a history student of BUK known as Siasia was stabbed in the head, and a law student from Edo State University, Nosa Osarumese had his ankle broken, in addition to a deep cut in the shoulder. They were rushed to the hospital for medical attention.

This was definitely the last straw. Delegates, at the behest of NANS leadership, packed their bags and left the campus, re-locating to Sabongari for safety. From there they made their way to Ahmadu Bello University, Zaria where the convention held peacefully and successfully. There a new NANS executive was elected. Ironically, the secretariat went to Bayero University. Constitutionally, it was the turn of the far north in the zone D of NANS to occupy the secretariat and BUK won. Now, the question being asked is what went wrong in BUK? Who were behind the attack on Nigerian students who were carrying out a normal activity in their own country?

The Vice Chancellor of BUK who went to the press penultimate Tuesday to announce the setting up of a panel to look into the cause of the crisis was nowhere to be found, while the disturbances on his campus lasted. Efforts by Academic Staff Union of Universities (ASUU) BUK branch and journalists to locate him proved abortive. Also the light and water supplies which were cut on the heels of the arrival of delegates were restored no sooner had the delegates left, as report has it.

Sources close to ASUU have it that the institution's authorities took a position on the convention to the effect that they could not play host to a "banned" organization's event contrary to ASUU's position that the convention should hold despite the ban. Also, the Mullahs were said to have been mobilised to ground all the convention activities as the delegates were alleged to be coming to wine and have fun with their ladies.

Curiously enough, the perpetrators of the acts of violence, according to reliable sources belong to a certain tribe. It was also gathered that the whole attack was as a result of a top level conspiracy. The conspiracy theory is reinforced by the allegation that a certain student of the Nigeria Law School came all the way from Lagos to lead the operation.

At present, the Hausa Muslims in Kano are said to be irked by the occurrence which they claim has dented the image of their state as a progressive one, moreso as non-indigenes are believed to have committed the mayhem.

XIV

THE DAYS OF THE DRACULA

[1996]

ONCE upon a time, the area around the Niger area which flows majestically from the hills of Futa Jallon was inhabited by different species of monsters. There were vermin, dragons, ogres and Draculas. They shared a common characteristic—they were misanthropes. They hated anything human though they had human skin. Each of these monsters reigned in the area at different times. Each reign was one of bloodletting and each potentate tried to outdo his predecessor in chilling murderous adventures. They consumed brothers, sisters, sons and daughters as well as visitors in their savage orgies. In this way, the area came to be known as Golgotha of the Niger Area where Lucifer, son of Morning held sway and the angels of the One from on high trembled and bowed.

Ironically, the Almighty God at creation was generous to a fault. He endowed the area with black gold, diamond, tin, marble, iron ore and uranium among others. These minerals were sealed with a lush vegetation like the Garden of Eden or Valley of Eskol. It was the envy of aliens who wished they were so gifted by Him who was at creation. These blessings were a curse for the people in this area as they were at the receiving end. The endowments were a force of attraction which brought each time to the saddle the monsters.

The reigns of the Ogre and Dracula were memorable. Their subjects would never forget them for a long time. The Ogre had an ever-smiling profile which won him acolytes who assisted him in his orgy of violence. His gap-tooth gave him away as a monster. He loved blood so much that he dreamt of eternal reign. His dream of eternity made him feast on his imagined enemies including his acolytes and would-be successors. He took some of his enemies to the sky with man-made bird and then drowned them in the swampy waters of the Niger Area. He was enamoured of the Bar Beach Show where humans were sacrificed to the sacred order of the Atlantic waters. So many of his acolytes were tools of sacrifice in the show. One of them used to muse and his story had a bow-leg. For this reason, the ogre sacrificed him to His Royal majesty, Okun, the god of the Atlantic. The cries of his miserable subjects ascended up to heaven and the creator in the grail temple heard and was moved. He afflicted the ogre with a disease of the foot and caused him to be removed from the throne. The angels did obeisance while earthmen revelled in bouts of happiness. This happiness did not endure. The Almighty only taught them a lesson: that He is the Most High and the strivings of earthmen are temporal before Him.

For the original sin of man, he would still make people of the Niger Area realise that He is Lord. So he gave them Dracula who had dour looks with tribal ornate. He loved wearing dark goggles. He was always depressed and came on only after sucking blood. First and foremost, on his ascent to the throne he mowed down two hundred of his subjects as burnt offering for demanding an end to the reign of monsters. The fickle-minded among his subjects who wished to save their necks offered to serve in his mill. They helped him in his bloody business—helping him to find, fix and finish. In homage, the minions would say: we will die for the Dracula! The Dracula is the centre of the kingdom! He is the alpha and omega! The only one that can keep the Niger Area together as one! The Dracula in his fury boasted that he would continue to rule even if he were alone in the Golgotha. When some of his subjects heard this warning, they struggled and scampered out of the Niger Area through the open windows of Benin, Niger, Cameroun into the refugee camps of Germany, United Kingdom, North America, Belgium, France, Italy and Canada among other safe havens where tales of the orgies of the Dracula are told in searing prose, drama and poetry. Among the exiles was a man who in times past passed a vote of no confidence on some white monsters who ravaged the Niger Area and named it so.

The Dracula was not happy that his subjects with good sinews, robust cheeks, grey hairs, swollen tommy, and long beard had escaped. He took precaution and so herded those who were left into dungeons. He then moved to sacrifice his subjects, precious tools of sacrifice to soothe his bloody appetite. In this manner, his subjects, namely, Yoruba, Ogoni and Itsekiri were consumed in a feast of fury that saw his acolytes in oratory of justifications. When this feast took place, white aliens who had at different times played host to the Dracula told him that the feast was simply unnecessary. He snapped and said he was the sovereign of the Niger Area, brooking no nonsense from anybody.

Craving as ever, he went to the dungeons of Abakaliki in Eboyin which harboured one of his subjects who sang songs of freedom. He made feast of him and strewed about his carcass. His subjects were outraged and feared that doing nothing about their fate, they would all find themselves in dishonourable graves. They stooped to ponder Like Shakespeare's Cassius:

…Rome, thou hast lost the breed of noble bloods!
When went there by an age
Since the great flood
But it was famed with more than one man?
When could they say, till now, that talked of Rome,
That her wide walls encompassed but one man?

They were comforted and strengthened in the fact that good would always triumph over evil. The days for them were that of the Dracula; their days would soon dawn and like Shakespeare's Cinna, they would proclaim:

Liberty! Freedom! Tyranny is dead!

XV

WHAT A COUNTRY

[PEMIUM TIMES ONLINE, MAY 27, 2015]

LET me confess that I am in a choleric humour and simultaneously weeping inside. Thus, in writing this piece, words are failing me. Truly, what can I say that no one has not said about the Nigerian condition? My friend and compatriot in the struggle against military dictatorship, Mr. Kunle Ajibade, Executive Editor of *The News* magazine, who spent some years at Makurdi prison for being accessory after the fact of a coup d'état titled his last reflections on the Nigerian question, *What a Country*. The pains that the rulers of Nigeria have inflicted on the Nigerian people are immeasurable that one cannot help longing for that day that the people will take their pound of flesh from their traducers; a revolution to consume the bashers of our collective destiny. Not the banalised version so-called 'silent revolution' but classical revolution whose dreadful aspect William Shakespeare captured so well in his *Julius Caesar*:

> *A curse shall lie upon the limbs of men;*
> *Domestic fury and fierce civil strife*
> *Shall cumber all the parts of Italy:*
> *Blood and destruction shall be so in use,*
> *And dreadful objects so familiar*
> *That mothers shall but smile when they behold*
> *Their infants quarter'd with the hands of war;*
> *All pity chok'd with custom of fell deeds:*
> *And Caesar's spirit, ranging for revenge,*
> *With Ate by his side, come hot from hell,*
> *Shall in this confines, with a monarch's voice,*
> *Cry 'havoc!' and let slip the dogs of war,*
> *That this foul deed shall smell above the earth*
> *With carrion men, groaning for burial.*

No! Nothing short of a revolution. In the last couple of weeks so much pain has been inflicted on the Nigerian people that upon contemplation, I kept muttering to myself, 'what a country'. Just visit any local market and see the long faces that market women and their customers wear. Or the anguish of those queuing for fuel at the filling station or the sufferings of commuters who have to pay exorbitant fares through their nose and the nuisance value of blocked thoroughfares by those queueing for fuel. Add this to the all-time low electricity supply. It is so bad. It is so sad. Quite frankly, we have had it to the hilt. Something just has to be done or else worse days will endure.

In the aftermath of the last general election, *The Guardian*, flagship of the Nigerian print media wrote a three-part editorial, titled *Nigeria on the rise*. The paper felt no matter the degree of contradictions of the Nigerian state, patriotism calls for the inspiring of hope in the people. It knew fully well that the elections have not changed the fundamentals of the Nigerian state: a country without a national creed—a no man's land peopled by homophobic and sadist species; a country with a substructure that is rentier and accumulation process that is largely primitive; a country with an elite who love the best in the world and loathe their replication in their own country; a thieving elite made up of ceremonial fops and parvenus who now owns sizeable percent of the choicest properties in central London investing about £250 million on property per annum and have also bought up a huge chunk of the apartments in Dubai and numerous others in other climes with fleets of private jets to boot. Contrast that with the sufferings of our people: Over 70 percent live on less than $2 per day, over 10 million of our children are out of school, empty ivory towers and broken infrastructures and multiple social crimes, a raging insurgency in the north east and the failure of two thirds of the states of the federation to pay workers salary. The Nigerian condition is so bad that even corpses lying in the streets are further abjectified by the refusal of state institutions to perform their statutory duties.

The latest exploit of this elite is the tightening of their stranglehold on the country through the oil scam, so-called subsidy. The country has become a victim of its blessing through the activities of this warped and backward elite in the name of oil subsidy, a mathematic fiction, and drainpipe through which they have milked the country dry in the last five decades. The oil racketeers, I mean marketers, are claiming that the incumbent federal government, its collaborator in the pillaging of the country, owes them some arrears of unpaid subsidy. This has become the basis for shutting down the country ahead of the inauguration of a new leadership in a bizarre manner never seen in the history of this country. Issues have come to a climax in which Nigerians can no longer access fuel and the product now sell as much as ₦500 per litre with a spiralling inflationary effect. Simultaneously, the ever epileptic electricity supply, has seized completely to gasp in the hands of the state looters who acquired them in the guise of privatisation with generous subsidy as well as un-incurred cost recovering tariff. Many who have bore-holes cannot pump water, food storage in the deep freezer and charging of handsets have become impossible. If this is a blackmail to continue the pillaging order, it will not work, we can't take it anymore. No more!

This change must be meaningful. This oil noose on our neck is inexplicable and absurd at a time when both the spot price and futures have remained on the downside. What sort of economic law is it that dictates quite absurdly that a country must pay international pricing for a product in which it has economy of scale? Put in another way, what sort of economic logic dictates that a country's natural endowment must be accessed and used by the owning country at international pricing? Such warped thinking can only come from the development set staffed by neoliberal ideologues. The latest noise from those patrons of poverty as I called them in a recent work came from Christine Lagarde, Managing Director, the International Monetary Fund (IMF) that Nigeria must be courageous to do away with oil subsidy. We will do away with oil subsidy not according to the prescription of the medicine men from IMF and the World Bank but because it does not exist; it is mere fraud. What a country!

XVI

THE STORY OF HOLLY AND JESSICA

[INSIDER WEEKLY, NOVEMBER 4, 2002]

OFTENTIMES, man's existential reality verges on the surreal or what some poets would call a hallucinatory dream. The disappearance of Holly Wells and Jessica Chapman, two British teenagers and residents of Soham in Cambridgeshire began like a dream on August 4, when the two bosom friends after an interaction in Wells' house suddenly disappeared. Two weeks later, on August 18, they were found dead apparently cold-bloodedly murdered. Indeed, it was like a dream. When their bodies were found in a ditch in a wooded spot near a US Air Base, RAF Lakenheath, Suffolk, by a shocked gamekeeper, Keith Pryer, they were already decomposing and blending with mother earth. This condition made it impossible for the coroner to ascertain the manner of their death, issuing out a crisp report: "unascertained due to decomposition".

For the dead friends, all the British dallies waxed lyrical. *Daily Mail* mailed, "Grief of a town with a broken heart"; *The Times* told, "Holly and Jessica: agony goes on"; *The Express* expressed, "Agony goes on for parents"; *The Guardian* guarded, "Town in mourning for lost girls" and *The Sun* blazed, "A single rose, a million tears". The grief caused by this incident in England and Wales, knew no bounds. It is still nightmarish for quite a lot of people. The girls' parents, Nicola and Kelvin Wells and Sharon and Leslie Chapman are in terrible shock that only time can heal. Mr. Pryer is sure his discovery will haunt him for the rest of his life. The football teams Chelsea and Manchester observed minutes of silence for the twosome who donned red-coloured Manchester United shirts at the time they were last seen.

The hard-working and highly-motivated British police have caught up with the culprits. They are Ian Huntley, 28, school caretaker and fiancée, Maxine Carr, 25, teaching assistant. The former, was broken-hearted having been jilted by a former spouse, Claire and the latter with a bee tattoo on her left breast is described by Paul Selby, a former boyfriend as wild with insatiable appetite for sex. While Huntley is being examined at Rampton Hospital for mental illness in Nottinghamshire, after a claim of a previous mental breakdown when his wife left him a few weeks after their wedding years back, Carr, his accomplice lover who made a court appearance once to the accompaniment of boos from a miffed British public is being remanded at the Holloway Prison in North London.

Will these culprits escape justice? Time will tell. Huntley is being currently held under the British Mental Health Act 1983 haven been adjudged to be suffering from mental disorder. But if he is found out to be unfit to stand trial and permanently sectioned, the law could avail in favour of Huntley as he has the right to apply to a tribunal and pray for freedom. This sort of leeway has provoked the call for restoration of the death penalty which had been abolished since 1965 in the United Kingdom. Commentators like Peter Hitchens think that it is only the death penalty that can serve as a deterrent to the rising incidence of homicide and other gory killings that have reared their head in the UK. According to Hitchens, the abolition of the gallows has removed the claws from the British penal system. He wishes earnestly for its restoration since for him death penalty is a weapon of civilization.

Given the magnitude of homicidal waves in the UK, one is tempted to agree with Hitchen's solution. As revealed by Home Office figures, in 1990, there were 67 child killings; in 2000, the figure rose to 110; and in 2001, 583 children were kidnapped.

In bouts of anxiety, parents are now considering surgical operation for their children. It involves the insertion of microchips into the body tissue. In emergency situations, it will allow for easy location of missing wards timeously.

XVII

THE VIRGIN NIGHTMARE

[NOVEMBER 2008]

LAST month, the London School of Economics and Political Science (LSE) had invited prominent scholars around the world to interrogate the place of democracy in International Relations. I was the only African scholar in the pack who made a presentation. Apart from the boredom of liberal discourse, the programme went well and I was eager to return to the routine of my office and the welcoming arms of my family in Nigeria, especially as the winter was already flexing its muscles.

During this trip, I took Virgin Nigeria, a sad reminder of the burst Nigerian Airways. The outward leg of my trip was without hitch except for the poor in-flight entertainment—the television was viewed on a blurred central screen. Therefore, I could not have imagined or envisaged in the least a delayed return flight much less outright cancellation. In the early hours of October 31, I set out from John Ruskin in South East London for Victoria Station to board the Gatwick Express coach with my bags and baggage containing mostly books and a few Christmas clothes for my children. As usual with most Nigerian affairs, I met a mass of passengers queuing to check in at the airport and I joined in. Almost, immediately, something not unusual in the air business happened; news spread to the effect that flight VK292 had been cancelled. Surprising, because there was no previous warning of this development. Infact, those who could not fly during the week had been assured of a flight on that day. The surging angry crowd drew the attention of the airport security and control personnel were brought to ensure order in the Virgin Nigeria check-in counter whose team could not offer us any intelligible reason for the cancellation. They were at their wit's end—no more suasion and confidence. What they lacked in utterance found vent in a note which stated that the airline's Boeing 767 long haul aircraft was away on 'scheduled maintenance checks' and passengers were assured of flight the next day, November 1. I was not convinced and not a few took the explanation with a pinch of salt. If this was the case, why were passengers some of whom came all the way from Manchester, looped? As if to vitiate our skepticism, we were offered accommodation at the five-star Gatwick Hilton and checked in ahead of the next day. A fifty percent discount on a future Virgin Nigeria flight within the next twelve months was also offered. These somewhat calmed the anger on the part of many. The offers made no impression on me. In point of fact, I was not ready to spend a day longer in London as I had planned my November ahead in ways to avoid being caught up in the Christmas rush.

The other side of the truth, however, was that a great number of the passengers jumped at the opportunity to stay in the cozy environment of Hilton. In its welcome pack was a three-square buffet. Since I was not normally resident in the United Kingdom, a factor that combined with hope of a flight the next day, I elected to stay at the hotel. Once in, I got glued to the television, catching up on the full coverage of the US elections to while away time. The consensus on the African-American Barrack Obama to the US presidency was infectious.—pundits called it media coronation.

By 10 p.m. that day, our predicament reached at once a level both of suspense and climax. An unidentified caller informed us that our flight for the next day had also been cancelled and that we would be well catered for by the hotel. To make it official, sometime around midnight, a formal notice to that effect was slid into our rooms. We were informed that flight VK292 had been rescheduled to depart on Monday, November 3 and further re-assured of a pleasant stay at Gatwick Hilton. The long wait had begun and anxiety was high. How long would this last? The hotel concierge had no answer. He in fact told me on enquiry that he merely told us what he was asked to communicate to the passengers. My mind fluttered between buying a one–way ticket home and waiting endlessly. Although the money I had on me could buy a ticket home, all of it was not mine—a large chunk of it was the usual diasporic transfer. I decided to endure the uncertain stay.

The second day dawned. Those who were enjoying the five star treat decided to invite to the hotel their friends who generously partook in the buffet that was not tightly controlled. Nevertheless, the caterers discovered that consumption had perhaps beaten their estimate and decided the next day to serve the Nigerian passengers by themselves. The trauma was not that they had to serve us by dishing into our plates but the quality of what they served was low and the choices limited. Everybody grumbled over this turn of event but there was no knowing whether all noticed the abuse of the process by some of the passengers. I recall a woman who asked the caterer, a male, to put a bit of chilli source in her food. He used his fingers to scoop it into her plate and I heard the woman complained sharply: 'don't use your hand'.

On Sunday evening, November 2, we got a firm commitment that we would fly the next day, Monday, November 3 and that wakeup call would come at 4.30 a.m. In anticipation, the passengers scurried for the trolleys and moved them into their rooms in readiness for departure the following morning. I was not carried away by this euphoria; I was doubtful. I reasoned that the notice was a ploy to quit us from the hotel in which not a few believed had eaten deep into the pause of the airline.

As it turned out, we the doubting Thomases were wrong. As early 3 a.m., some of the passengers had queued up at the check-in counter. The queue was a long one but we all boarded. While air borne, a hundred percent discount letter on the next Virgin Nigeria flight supplanting the earlier one, was distributed to all the passengers. You need to imagine the excitement that greeted this gesture. Shouts of 'praise the Lord, Alleluia' echoed about the aircraft. This was intensified as the airplane which hovered for almost an hour came to a downy halt at Murtala Mohammed Airport.

XVIII

IF THEY PLAY JAZZ IN HEAVEN, PLAY ON DIZZY

[THE GUARDIAN, JANUARY 9, 1993]

IN these parts, the news of the death of African American Jazz trumpeter, John Birks (Dizzy) Gillespie was received with great shock and heavy hearts by his numerous admirers. Reminiscences of his last outing here apparently flowed in the minds of many who were fortunate to watch the music virtuoso perform on stage. They would remember his Sextet comprising Giovana Hildago (Conga), John Lee (Bass) Ed Cherry (guitar) Ignacio Berroa (drums) James Moody (Saxaphone); they would remember such numbers as Theolonos Monks' *Round Midnight*, Moody's *Mood for Love* and *Night in Tunisia* performed by them; and they would of course remember Gillespie's swollen cheeks when he blew the trumpet with great dexterity that is *Bebop* of which he was the master and innovator. The University of Lagos community, especially the Centre for Cultural Studies would be hard hit because when he performed there four years ago, precisely January 25, 1989, the 2000 capacity Main Auditorium brimmed with a turn-out of students and staffers who literally went wild as Gillespie churned out popular tunes from his rich repertoire. I could recall Dr. Alaja-Browne of the Centre for Cultural Studies describing his performance as "brightest".

Before he ended his visit to Nigeria which was at the instance of the United States Information Agency (USIA), he was invested with the title: *Bashere of Iperu*, by Oba Joseph Ogunfowora, the Alaperu of Iperu, Ijebu-Remo. I can actually recall his jokes, "When I told my wife I have been made a chief on the phone, she said to me: 'you know what to do with yourself'", he said humorously.

Gillespie regarded as one of the great masters of jazz is perhaps the last of the titans, from a long pedigree beginning from the early 20s with such names as the great trumpeter, Louis 'Satchmo' Armstrong; composer and New Orleans celebrated ragtime pianist, Ferdinand "Jelly Roll" Morton; Empress of the Blues, Betty Rose, Mile Davis, Charles Tolliver; Thomas Torrentine, James Cleveland…*et al.*

Gillespie did a lot to promote the African-American music genre—Jazz—a fact that made the US Congress remark that jazz 'is a rare and valuable American treasure." US congressman Conyer therefore sought for it a national recognition through its institutionalisation. This compliment is also a testimony to the dynamic essence of jazz from *ragtime* to *swings* and *blues*, and gravitation towards formalization. Its acceptability is no doubt due to its fundamental message. This message was aptly put by Ben Tomoloju in a commentary on roots jazz festival in *The Guardian* March 19, 1988.

"It was a message from the distant, from the plantation in the slavery days when this freedom stressing music has at its inchoate stages, serving as a spiritual tranquiliser, social equilibrating and therapeutic agent for children of Africa dislodged from their roots". This essence has also taken on contemporaneous manifestations in a dynamic world. Again, Tomoloju says it all. "Even on stage, you feel it. In the church liturgies, the red-light districts of pub-crawlers, among intellectuals, it rings bell when the modern day acolytes mount the platform".

Gillespie had numerous performances. He appeared at jazz workshop, San Francisco American Monterey Jazz Festival California, Juan-Les-Pins Festival, France including music life of Charlie Parker which made an outing in both Eastern and Western Europe. He also represented United States' department on culture in a tour of Iran, Pakistan, Lebanon,

Syria, Turkey, Yugoslavia, Greece and South Africa between 1950-56. Gillespie won so many music awards including first prize soundtrack Berlin Film Festival, Downbeat Critics Poll Award, Handel Medallion, American National Music Award and the prestigious Grammy Award which he won in 1975,. He bagged an honorary Doctorate degree from Rutgers University in the US. Gillespie's popular numbers include, *Jazz for Sunday afternoon; Trumpet kings at Monteux JF; Having a good time in Paris*, among others.

The Bebop master died of cancer on Wednesday at the age of 75 and, may, perhaps play jazz in heaven. He was born at Cheraw, South Carolina, October 21, 1917. He graduated from Laurinburg Institute, North Carolina. He is survived by wife, Lorraine Willis and two sons, James and Lottie.

XIX

FOR CARLOS FUENTES AND OLAITAN OYERINDE

[THE GUARDIAN, MAY 23, 2012]

TWO important people died recently. They are the Mexican novelist and leftist Carlos Fuentes and Comrade Olaitan Oyerinde. The former died a fulfilled old man at 83 on May 15 in faraway Mexico and the latter died in brutal circumstances at 44 on May 5 in Benin City. Olaitan was shot dead by assassins acting out the orders of hooded misogynists in the presence of his wife and children at the Ugbo area of the city. I remember both for what they stood for while living.

I never met Fuentes except in the imagined world of his essay through which I became emotionally attached to him. Intriguingly, I read only one of his essays published in *Transition* in 1991 and never read any of his novels. The essay titled, "The End of Ideologies?" is a reflection on the immediate post-bipolar world. Fuentes warns against the festivities in the West over the collapse of communism and the projection of capitalism as the end of history and of course the end of diversity. Socialism fossilised due to the absence of self-criticism, he argues. It however fulfilled a socialisation role for capitalism by its incessant criticism of the capitalist mode of production. He goes to say there is no such thing as pure capitalism and the state has continued to play a socialising role for capital by its periodic intervention to regulate vagrant capital. He further reminds us that: "The most serious of social problems have not vanished with the festivities of 1989 and 1990. Whatever these festivities have celebrated hardly offsets those tendencies that from now on must be kept under critical check and resolved by a process of the socialisation of political life. In other words: the end of Stalinism east of the Elba River does not mean the end of social injustice west of that river, nor, for that matter, north or south of the Bravo River." For the United States he has a message: "The U. S., so intent on finding enemies outside its borders that suit the Manichean script of its historical record, will have to deal with its internal enemies. Among them: the lack of women's rights, ecological ruin, educational bankruptcy, the drying up of funds for scientific research, crumbling bridges and roads, blighted cities in the throes of drugs and violence, the plight of the elderly and the homeless, millions living under the 'poverty line.'"

For his beloved region of Latin America, he says the social changes that occurred were as a result of the labour of the left and reminds them of their historical obligation for social justice, and organising from the bottom up will help this where market theology and its trickledown effect never materialised.

Above all, Fuentes envisages a multi-culture 21st century, and perhaps never envisages the fight back of nationalism and racist forces. He will be right eventually because despite these forces, the ones at work in the new century such as the communication revolution is headed towards multiculturalism. Earthmen will learn to live side by side with different cultures and synthesise new ones. Anything else may well mean the reversal of humanity to the precarious edge of pre-history.

Going through those reflections, Fuentes immediately came across as a progressive person with pro-left ideas though some critics called him a 'moderate liberal'. Bill Swainson, Fuentes' British editor described him as "one of the most extraordinary writers in an extraordinary generation that included Gabriel García Márquez, Julio Cortázar and Mario Vargas Llosa. Together the 'Boom' generation, as they came to be known, reinvented the novel in Latin America and made it into a force that commanded international attention." Some of his works include *Aura* (1962) and *The Death of Artemio Cruz* (1962) *The Old Gringo* (1985 and *Diana, The Goddess Who Hunts Alone (1994).*

The second subject, Olaitan was my schoolmate and comrade at the University of Lagos (UNILAG). We came into the institution in the same year 1987. He came through direct entry and I through the Joint Matriculation Examination. We both came in as already socialised Marxists, not learning the ropes. At twenty three, I was a mature student and a stringer with *The Guardian* Arts Desk after haven had a brief spell at the Nigerian Institute of Journalism. Olaitan was in the Department of Mass Communication and I in History. Gbenga Olawepo and I shared bed space at Shodeinde Hall and Olaitan spent a lot of time with us. During the same period, late Comrade Bala Jubril Mohammed joined us as a post-graduate student in the Department of Mass Communication and we then inaugurated the Marxist-Leninist Study Group (MLSG). We met on Sundays. In a manner of speaking, it was our Sunday School. Most of the critical ideas, I have in me today were milled in that school, not in the classroom. The Unilag we met had no union. It was the aftermath of the 1986 students' crisis and the consequent Abisoye panel conditionalities. Those of us in MLSG and our comrades in the Socialist Youth League (SYL) staged a demonstration at the Senate Building and demanded the resuscitation of the Students' Union. This was granted and a moderate Philip Madojutimi became the president of the union in 1988.

In 1989, I was fielded as Presidential Candidate of the left as replacement for Comrade Juliet Southey-Cole, a female candidate who had strong followership, and this for two reasons. Her chances were annulled by a *force majeure.* The anti-SAP protest of 1989 shut down the Babangida regime and equally led to the closure of some campuses for six months. With the time lag, I was the only eligible leftist candidate with the required grade point aggregate for students' union leadership. I was at 200 level and others were in their final year and could not be fielded. We had a strong campaign organization in which Olaitan, Amos Abiodun Ayodele, Victor Ukaogo, Gbenga Olawepo, and Raskey Ojikutu, Patrick Ubulu, Late Rotimi Ewebiyi, Anslem Iyoha, Segun Abifarin and many others played important roles. On Election Day, Olaitan drove the standby 504 Peugeot car that that was secured by us for the exercise, shuttling between Akoka and Idi-Araba campuses of the University. Such was the culture of commitment in which we were raised. In his final year, Olaitan gave me his bed space at El-kanemi Hall and joined Gbenga Olawepo at Henry Carr Hall. In between, we shared food and everything. We never asked the question: where do you come from? As Internationalists, we believed in the unity of the oppressed people everywhere in the world. It is the same Internationalist spirit that took Olaitan to Edo state. If ethnicity was a factor in our lives, as it has become today, Olaitan would have declined to work with Adams Oshiomhole in Edo.

We had dreams, dreams of a Nigerian Revolution. I moved into the burgeoning pro-democracy movement right from school without working in a private or public establishment. Olaitan moved into the Iron and Steel Senior Staff Association of Nigeria (ISSAN). Let me recall that Olaitan and I lived in the same room at Iyana Ipaja area of Lagos. I had become the General Secretary of the Campaign for Democracy and was in hiding in his place when General Abacha let loose his hounds and I was subsequently arrested and moved to Birnin Kebbi Prison. While Olaitan was in Benin, we hardly met. We had lunch together at the Benin Airport when I ran into him waiting for his principal who had just lost his wife in 2010. He was not the violent type. He was an intellectual and thus very critical. Those values he brought to bear on Adams Oshiomhole administration. I do not know the motive of those who murdered him. As a non-indigene, he was not aspiring to be a commissioner or governor of the state. He probably wanted to go back to the Nigerian Labour Congress. The mindless killing of this great man is the height of barbarism. Let me end with the words of Fuentes: "There must be something beyond slaughter and barbarism to support the existence of mankind and we must all help search for it."

XX

JUST TO SAY GOOD BYE

[THE GUARDIAN, FEBRUARY 10, 2011]

DEATH "a necessary end, will come, when it will come." These are the eternal words of William Shakespeare in his dramatic piece, *Julius Caesar*. I have accepted the fact that one day I will bid good bye to earthly men and women; and this is so etched deep in my consciousness that I wrote my will in the nasty days of the Abacha regime when I held forth as General Secretary of the foremost pro-democracy movement in Nigeria, the Campaign for Democracy, in its heydays. Oh ubiquitous death! I lost a number of friends to the cold fingers of death in the year gone by. They were not only my friends but friends of Nigeria in that they had laboured for this country so that it can be and its people can be human. The roll call included Arc. Babatunde Kuye, Ms. Adetoun Adeloye and Chief Anthony Enahoro. I crossed the path of these great people, great Nigerians all, in the course of my service to humanity.

Late 2005, I moved into a new abode at Agbara Estate, Ogun State with my family, the oldest private estate, perhaps in West Africa. I immediately took interest in the activities of the estate. I participated in its monthly meetings where the welfare of the residents and the estate are the regular subject of discussion. By 2008, there was leadership vacuum in the residents association. Having spent the greater part of my youth in activism; I was a bit reluctant to assumed leadership position in the running of the residents association. Previously, I had served quietly in its Anniversary Committee and this time I was elected to serve in the Interim Management Committee (IMC) for two months as Secretary and Kuye, Chairman. The latter had served as chairman of the association before and it was out of commitment to the interest of the residents that he agreed to lead the organisation until a proper executive was constituted. Between February and April of that year, Kuye, the famous architect, put in a lot of energy into the running of the organization; there was hardly any week that the IMC did not hold one or two meetings. He was forceful for his age and goal-oriented. He brought humour to bear on the proceedings at our meetings and had a partner in mirthful Chief BD Okpomor. Within the two months we served the Residents Association, we bought a bus for the security unit, bolstered the security in the estate, shored up the collection of service charge and won interest and participation of the largely disinterested residents. Kuye took ill and later joined his ancestors last July. I left Benin City to join mourners at his grave side in Ikoyi cemetery to say good bye.

Adetoun Adeloye was the cheerful presenter of *Day Time Talk*, a current affairs programme on the Lagos Television, Ikeja. I was introduced into her acquaintance sometime in 2006 as a potential speaker in her programme by my bosom friend, Osa Director, former Editor-in-Chief of *Insider Weekly*. From then on, we became good friends. She was like an elder sister to me, even though I do not know her exact age. A single parent with children, she had challenges that went with that status. She could confide in me. She loved her job and as with most occupations in Nigeria there was no commensurate reward. Whenever she had no discussant for her programme she would call on me and often I obliged by being present or inviting someone else as a replacement. With a scholarly disposition, she often asked me to suggest topics for discussion. She passed on last August. She was last seen in her office on Friday August 13 and probably died in her apartment that weekend of unknown cause (I do not have the autopsy report). She was found dead and in bad condition, when anxious friends and neighbours broke into her apartment. Truly, Toun died out of frustration with the lie of things in our country. There was no home she could call her own; no good salary. She had to cope with the demands of her job and as a single parent—the triple burden of being a professional, mother and breadwinner. This woman started her career in the 1980s as a broadcaster at the Ondo State Broadcasting Corporation, had a brief turn at the Murtala Mohammed Airport as International Flight Announcer and ended up at the Lagos Television. Although, I was not able to pay graveside homage, it is never too late to say goodbye.

Last December, Chief Anthony Enahoro (Mr. Independence) joined his ancestors. In July, on his last birthday, I visited him at his Aideyan Avenue residence, Government Reservation Area, Benin City. During that visit I apologised to him that I could not make his press briefing in Lagos. Papa was looking frail and he told me such was life. I never had a close relationship with papa but he had some admiration for my activism in a country with a dwindling tribe of activists who know its dynamics and competing social forces. Even at my age, I live with a morbid fear of our inability to reproduce ourselves. It was for this reason that I grieved over the exit of Chief Gani Fawehinmin. Although, nature abhors vacuums, sometimes, it takes a generation, or even a century to fill certain vacuums. In the case of Papa, his resilience in the struggle was outstanding. He began as a radical youth and moved the independence motion in 1953 at the age of 29. Like Moses to Pharaoh, he told the British 'let my people go.' He went to prison several times and with the outbreak of the civil war, he served in the Gowon regime and had some romance with the politicians of the Second Republic, returning to activism in the 1990s with the deepening of authoritarianism in the country.

It was during the 1990s that I became an ally of Pa Enahoro. When I was arrested by the regime of Abacha in January of 1995, and held incommunicado with no public knowledge of my whereabouts, he took it upon himself to go to court to compel the military to produce me. He also organised some relief materials for my dependants. By the time I was released in 1996, it was papa's turn again to return to exile like the fugitive offender that he was in the 1960s. As a fugitive offender, Papa's odyssey had spurned a colloquial expression in Ghana. Indeed, students of the University of Ghana at Legon, were habituated to threatening themselves with the act of being *enahoroed*. When Pa Enahoro went into exile in the late 1990s until his return in 2000, it was not a sweet experience. He suffered the deprivations and humiliation of a non-income earner all for the sake of Nigeria. In 1998, I was in Aachen, Germany, when the Kunle Animashaun-led Congress of Nigerian Democrats in Germany (CONDIG) sent him medication in the United States. For this colossus of our historical annals, I say goodbye and may the Nigeria of your dream be.

XXI

REQUIEM FOR BULLET STONER

[THE GUARDIAN, JULY 28, 2011]

EACH time I reflect on life on earth, with all the daily toils, I marvel about its meaning. Life on earth is a reality that we cannot change until Armageddon occurs whether in the prophetic way as in the holy writ or through the destructive acts of man. Today, the split atoms in the arsenal of the superpowers can destroy the home of man over and over again. We are already reaping the consequences of abuse of mother earth through man's emission of greenhouse gases. The struggle is between light and darkness. The capacity to overcome the dark recesses of ones being, beaming light on it in ways that enhance the humanity of others is perhaps the pearl of life. It does not lie in the overwhelming acquisition of the material things of life.

A few weeks ago, Johnbull Enaboifo, also known as Dr. Bullet Stoner, bade goodbye to mother earth and those of us still struggling to know and overcome it. He performed his rite of departure exactly on July 5, after a failed fight with almighty death. Life and death are two mysteries in our world. To re-echo the lyrics of Christy Ogba, death remains man's dilemma, and it cannot be appeased. Our subject here lived a peculiar life; peculiar because it was different from the normal social order of the cultural surroundings. He was always friendly with the product of barley and malt. In a manner of speaking, he was friends with the bottle. He loved the content of the bottle more than the best of African dishes one could put on the table. He was not particularly selective with spirit, and again in a manner of speaking, he was a man of all weather. However, in this social deviancy, lay his virtue; he was fearless and could tell you to kill him if you could and that he was not afraid to die. He trod where the angels feared. Having gained freedom from fear in ways conceived by Auug San Suu Kyi, the Myanmar iron lady who is fighting authoritarianism in her country, he was really free to say anything he felt like. In many ways, he spoke the truth which many in the normal social mode could not. He said those things that were not pleasant to the ear, serving them raw to his interlocutor or audience. Whenever, he fired his bullet, he would cushion them with peals of laughter; laughter so infectious, that one could not help laughing. Often when he told the truth, he took oath in the name of man and God to drive home his point and sincerity. He must have realised that truth and justice "are often the only bulwarks which stand against ruthless power" that is also evident in his local milieu.

Bullet Stoner, as he was fondly called, crossed my path during my participation in the last primaries of the Action Congress of Nigeria (ACN) to represent Esan Central, Esan West and Igueben Federal Constituency in the Federal House of Representatives. He supported me and not because I was a money bag, but because he believed I could make a difference. In his support for me he did what a thousand megaphones could not do. On his lips and with his weary eyes open, he would shout my name at every opportunity. And on the day of the primaries, he stood in front of me to demonstrate the fact that he was there for me. Again, he had commitment, another great virtue you could hardly find anywhere, very rare among the governing class in our country.

Although a social deviant, he had a wife and children, one of whom lives overseas. His wife lived with him until his last day. Professionally, he was an electrical engineer who graduated from Auchi Polytechnic and he knew the job very well. There were those who derided him as stupid and useless, but in death he shared the glory which William Shakespeare reserved only for princes. The English dramatist once wrote in his epic drama,

Julius Caesar that "when beggars die, there are no comets seen, the heavens themselves blaze forth the death of princes." You may wonder if our beloved Bullet Stoner was a prince. Yes he was one; he hailed from the royal quarters of Ekpoma. You might have thought him a beggar, as I believe many in Ekpoma where he lived did all because of his life style as a social deviant much in love with the bottle. For me, he was not a beggar; he was only a social deviant, but also an outstanding personality who spoke the truth all times whether before kings or ordinary people. If Bullet believed in a course, he would pursue it with all his might; such was his commitment. To use the words of Vaclav Havel, the former Bulgarian Prime Minister, he was an example of the power of the powerless. And to add my voice, he was a salient but ignored conscience of his community. He will be fondly remembered by all of us who share his values. Adieu!

XXII

A TRIBUTE TO A BRAVE COUPLE

[DECEMBER 2012]

YULETIDE was forthcoming and as usual everyone was caught up in the hustle and bustle of preparations. You were not left out. As it was your tradition, you wanted to take your family elsewhere, in other words, change environment for familial bonding. There was always a certain air and feeling of freedom and attendant inexplicable health implication; somewhat therapeutic, whenever you did. Therefore you eagerly looked forward to, shall we say, this other lease of life. A few days to this Christmas, however, you were suddenly overwhelmed with an uncanny feeling of doubt as to whether you should travel for the season's holiday or not. You told your expectant family members in a patriarchal pitch that you were no longer travelling out of your normal place of abode, in this case Agbara and Lagos.

You then planned to alter in some creative way, the drudgery of being in the same environment. You would take the children and madam to Muson Centre on the eve of Christmas day for a start to watch Odia Ofeimun's *Nigeria the Beautiful* and the *Feast of Return*. Felix Okolo's stage chorography would be something to thrill the young ones and nurture in them a sense of the aesthetics. This first level plan looked realist and was thus sealed. However, a day before the eve, at about 5 p.m., you got a call from your friend and comrade who broke the news of the sudden transition of a comrade of yours and family friend. Still in shock, you were also told that his spouse was also a victim of the ritual of transition to the great beyond. Unbelieving, you inquired about the nature of the sudden transition. The man had arranged with his wife on the fateful day to pay homage to his in-laws at Ikoro-Ekiti, a town in Ekiti State. The wife normally lived in Ilorin and husband Osogbo. They had arranged that the wife should come over from Ilorin and wait at Omu-Aran and the husband, drive there from Osogbo in their onward journey to Ikoro. Both were happily united and made it to the wife's place and on their way back, somewhere in Iloro, few kilometres from Ido-Ekiti, the Hiace bus which they had travelled in, husband and wife occupying the front seats, somersaulted.

No one could tell in dramatic and minute detail what went wrong. The couple died on the spot and were conveyed by the Federal Road Safety Corps (FRSC) to the Federal Medical Centre (FMC) in Ido and deposited in the morgue. Still too incredible, confirmation from those who knew the couple was important. A close comrade in the vicinity assumed that office and confirmed in sobbing tones that the news was real. You decided there and then in company of a mutual friend to see things for yourself. You headed to the FMC and you saw the couple, friends you had wined and dined with lying lifeless; they were no more and had faded into history, to be referred to in the past tense. In a manner that drove home the reality of their transition and at once scaled up your sorrow, text messages poured in from sympathizers who knew how close you were to the departed. One read: "By overcoming the challenges that the fallout from the tragic death of Comrade and Mrs. Kolawole Abiodun you shall be soothed." Another read: "My brother, I didn't know what to say, and that is the reason why I didn't call you earlier." You were yet to be weaned of your sobbing bouts when fate again thrust on your laps the harrowing task of breaking the news of the death to the eldest son of the couple who was barely 15 years old. You could imagine your pains and while sobbing the following lines formed in your mind: *akha d' ukpon, e-eh ukpon so ma/ egbe na tete o la ki eken/ egbe kha yu, orion la bu onoyaen* (when you dress yourself in your fanciful clothes, you look good/ the body that you adore so well shall be sand someday/ and when the body ceases to be alive, your soul shall return to the creator).

The next stage was burial. Again, you accompanied the bodies to their final resting place—a twin grave and watched their coffins being lowered into them. As you left the grave side, you saw four sobbing children who could barely fend for themselves and the humanity in you gave way, with tears rolling down your cheeks, as a result.

This was my ordeal in this last season of festivities. It was for me a season of mourning and soul-searching. I lost a comrade and his better half, Abiodun Kolawole and Cecilia Temitayo Kolawole. A few words about this brave couple: As Frantz Fanon reminds us, "Each generation must, out of relative obscurity, discover its mission, fulfill it, or betray it." Comrade Abiodun Kolawole, 45, a former Secretary-General of the National Association of Nigerian Students (NANS) did not search for too long to discover what his mission was in the Nigerian wilderness. He saw the many contradictions of the society which had truncated many an aspiration and indeed produced many wasted generations. He joined early in life the band of idealists and revolutionary workers intent on enacting the Nigerian revolution. From the student movement to prodemocracy and self-determination struggles, he worked doggedly for the structural transformation of the Nigerian society. These activities were to drive him into exile in Cote d'Ivoire for a couple of years until the exit of the military in 1999. Comrade Kolawole was a revolutionary who would be remembered for his single-minded commitment to the cause of the transformation of Nigeria to a better place for all; his infectious humility and devotion to self-less service. He held the abiding belief that permanent struggle was important in order to preserve human liberty. He was in the vanguard of the struggle against IMF-World Bank inspired Structural Adjustment Programme (SAP) in Nigeria and was committed to the highest principle of revolutionary struggle demonstrated robustly in the struggle against military rule and the restoration of democracy.

Cecilia, 43, was a woman made in heaven, motherly, devoted and tolerant. As every revolutionary worker knows, without a woman committed to the struggle on the side of the man, the latter is more likely to derail, especially in the difficult environment that is Nigeria. This woman suffered many deprivations for the sake of the struggle to save Nigeria, a struggle to which her husband was married and to which by implication she was also wedded. She suffered the years of exile with her husband in Cote d'Ivoire and bore the greater part of the burden raising their children. It was not by accident that she died with the husband—it was a sacrifice of devotion.

Abiodun and Cecilia, you will continue to remain evergreen in our collective memory and consciousness. While we rise in proud salute to your courage, we pray that your children may inherit the future of your dreams.

XXIII

BEYOND WHISPERS, BABA GOES HOME

[OCTOBER 2013]

I received the news of Baba Oluwide Omojola's mortal passage with an indescribable shock. During his 75th birthday which held at Yard 158, Oregun, Ikeja, Lagos, I was the compeer of the occasion. Baba in what may now be regarded a premonition whispered to me how good it was for one to witness his/her funeral. Overwhelmed by the pool of well-wishers, Baba glimpsed a picture of the number of people that would attend his rites of transition in that event. Beyond whispers, Baba has now joined his ancestors.

I was one of Baba's many adopted children, from the point of view of the fatherly role he played in my tutelage as a revolutionary Marxist. I became class conscious in 1983 with my induction into a Marxist cell built by Blessed Isi Momodu at Ekpoma. Momodu had been converted at Ife by the Ife Collective comprising of Segun Osoba, Omotoye Olorode and Idowu Awopetu among others. On coming to Lagos in the mid-eighties, Baba and many other comrades opened up opportunities for me to excel and achieve greater ideological clarity. Baba's 24 Jebba Street office, Ebute Metta, haboured volumes of rare books and archival materials where several meetings such as the Movement for Popular Democracy (MPD) were held by us. We also had meetings in his rented apartment at The Lodge, 22 Itolo Street, Eric Moore, Lagos, especially at those times when efforts were being made to bring together all the revolutionary left organisations under the toga of Socialist Revolutionary Vanguard (SRV). Then I was in the Femi Ahmed-led Patriotic Labour Movement (PLM). We always thought the Nigerian revolution was next day. Despite the many revolution-provoking situations in the country, the subjective factor had never fully ripened and although many left organisations retreated into their sectarian shells, we remained in the SRV of which Baba was the leader after comrade Ola Oni died in 1999.

It is important to point out here how the bourgeois state reacts to security issues. In 1992, after the economic protest of May 14 and 15 described then by the military dictator, General Ibrahim Babangida, as the civilian equivalent of a military coup. Baba, Beko Ransome-Kuti, Gani Fawehinmin, Femi Falana and Segun Mayegun were arrested and detained at Kuje prisons. Ms. Bimbo Akinyemi and I were surprisingly left off the hook after being detained a couple of days at Area F, Ikeja. The first four aforementioned were unlawfully and unjustly detained as protests were coordinated by Segun Mayegun as NANS president, me and other comrades of the University of Lagos pursuant to a mandate given by the Senate of NANS to the secretariat (then headquartered at UNILAG) at its session at the University of Port Harcourt. The other Four except Mayegun never made any input. It was the students who were responsible for the action. Baba and the remaining were victimised mainly because of their anti-military stance.

Baba, the thinker made efforts to revive the *Massline*, a Marxist cadre journal, in order to promote critical thinking in the left and a section was created for basic theory. I recall his clarion call on this score in a letter dated August 14, 2001: "The consensus is that it is about time to restart our movement's theoretical journal. A theoretical journal is appropriate to strategise our options to confront inroads in the freedom of our world or minimally to expose the new slave drivers. Current postures and activities of the new imperialism imposing on us our historical duty of channeling our energies to renewing the world more gainfully can also be promoted by MASSLINE"

Again, tireless Baba along with other comrades made effort to revive the unity of the left on the platform of All-Nigeria Socialist Alliance (ANSA) of which Comrade Abiodun Aremu and I became joint interim secretary. Baba Omojola was one of the moving forces behind the Socialist Party of Nigeria (SPN). He and Comrade Jonathan Ihonde wanted a greater role for the successor generation--younger comrades. One hopes this comes to pass. Baba was a great thinker who had advanced the theory of primitive accumulation taking a cue from Marx and Engels in an unpublished work titled *Primitive Accumulation in Nigeria* and which I made efforts to publish through an appropriate channel while I was in London between, 2001-2004. Baba functioned in the faculty of the Centre for Constitutionalism and Demilitarization (CENCOD), especially in its governance training programme. He contributed a chapter titled "Fundamental Principles of Economic Policy: Application and Results in Nigeria" to *Governance: Nigeria and the World* which I edited in 2004.

He was personally close to my family. My wife, a Doctor of Optometry, took care of his eyes. She and I cajoled him into coming to spend some time with us in our Agbara abode which he obliged, making good the rare occasion to counsel us on marital matters. Occasionally, he found time to send phone credit to my eldest son who in a manner of speaking is his grandson. I had always lamented the fact that at his age he was doing things by himself. He drove himself about Lagos. We were supposed to take care of him. It is sad that I did not have enough means to fulfil that as a personal obligation. The love of my life, political economy, not bourgeois political economy, which focuses on the relations of things but the Marxist variant, whose method is the method of abstraction and interrogates the material conditions of society which underpins my scholarly endeavour, was a course I had intended to deepen through my association with Baba. I have lost that opportunity but I can assure Baba, I will not disappoint him. Although Olatunji Dare has rightly noted in a tribute (Farewell *to Baba and Omo*) that with his death, Nigeria's public sphere is poorer, we take solace in the hope that his ideas and values will not be put away with his bones. As Che Guevara once said, "Whenever death may surprise us, let it be welcome if our battle cry has reached even one receptive ear and another hand reaches out to take up our arms."